P9-DXI-553

WHAT CAN I WRITE ABOUT?

7000 TOPICS FOR HIGH SCHOOL STUDENTS

David Powell
Western New Mexico University

National Council of Teachers of English
1111 Kenyon Road, Urbana, Illinois 61801

For Maria

    again and ever

NCTE Editorial Board: Paul T. Bryant, Marilyn Hanf Buckley, Thomas J. Creswell, C. Kermeen Fristrom, Jane M. Hornburger, Robert F. Hogan, *ex officio*, Paul O'Dea, *ex officio*

Staff Editor: Barbara Davis

Book Design: Tom Kovacs

NCTE Stock Number 56568

Library of Congress Cataloging in Publication Data

Powell, David, 1934-
   What can I write about?

  1. English language—Composition and exercises.
2. Creative writing (Secondary education) I. Title.
II. Title: Topics for high school students.
LB1631.P66   808.042'0712   81-9675
ISBN 0-8141-5656-8   AACR2

CONTENTS

PREFACE

The question all composition students ask—
"What can I write about?"—is answered more
than 7,000 times in this volume. The teacher in
search of assignments can simply glance down
any page of a desired category of writing and
see countless ideas spring forth. Appeals are
made throughout the book to a comprehensive
range of interests, knowledge, experience, feelings, and thoughts; there is an abundance of
"something for everyone." Furthermore, the
mind being limitless, these topics passed on from
teacher to students should suggest to all students
(not just the inquisitive or imaginative ones) still
other ideas they can identify with, many of
which they may come up with on their own.

Certainly one of the first aims of teaching is
to bring students to self-discovery, and it is no
small accomplishment if, by looking outside,
students are brought to look within themselves.

Notes heading each of the chapters in *What
Can I Write About?* briefly define the different
kinds of writing, tell how to write them, and
indicate how the book may be used to locate
topics suited to them, leaving little need for
formal classroom instruction. The best (and
perhaps the happiest) teacher may be the one
who has the least to say.

David Powell
Western New Mexico University

DESCRIPTION

What Description Is

For our purposes here, we might say that to describe something—object, emotion, thought, event, and on over the horizon of human experience—is to surround it with written words, much the way lines shape the subject of a drawing. The Greek root of the word "scribe" is instructive. It means to scratch, or sketch an outline. That implied lightness of touch can be important. We should seek to surround our subject not so much to capture it (and least of all to annihilate it) as to liberate it, let it stand forth in a new fullness and freshness. Descriptive writing can free its subject from itself, from the obscurity of experience, and in the same stroke bear it to a life larger than the words surrounding it. The words should not draw attention to themselves; rather, they should scratch a descriptive network so tough and resilient it can spring the subject free of its own description.

How to Write Description

Good descriptive writing is first of all concrete. Search out the telling detail, the essential characteristic, then nail it down. But the warning above applies here as well: the subject must be nailed down without stabbing it to death. We are not out to pin dead dry bugs to a board. Keep them alive. Keep them moving. This is best done with verbs and nouns. When we run on to a chasm between the verb and the noun we can throw an adjective like a lifeline, or a bridge, between the two—always remembering, though, that such connections are seldom strong enough to support a sentence.

Here, from one of the familiar tales of the Brothers Grimm, is a simple illustration of how sensual descriptive writing should be:

> "Oh, Grandmother, what big ears you have,"
>   she said.
> "The better to hear with, my dear."
> "Grandmother, what big eyes you have."
> "The better to see with, my dear."
> "What big hands you have, Grandmother."
> "The better to hold you with, my dear."
> "But, Grandmother, what big teeth you have."
> "The better to eat you up with, my dear."
> Hardly had the Wolf said this, than he sprang from the bed and gobbled up poor little Red Riding Hood.

Poor Red Riding Hood indeed. She seems to have been lacking in one element vital to graphic description—imagination. But at least we can learn from the wolf. Let all descriptive writers put teeth in their words and gobble up the reader.

Locating Subjects for Description

Description is clearly one of the broadest kinds of writing. Just about any subject listed in this book could inspire a descriptive passage. Descriptive writing is, by way of example, sometimes fundamental to creative and narrative writing. This would, then, be an appropriate time to begin to regard this book as a whole and to move, by directing the assignments to students, freely from part to part. The subjects in the present chapter will be seminal for descriptive writing exercises of all kinds, but the book strives to become, as a whole, a descriptive network not unlike the one we have described above, outlining, however lightly, the power and possibility of writing.

Nature and Natural Settings

Describe:

a morning rain
a cottonfield sun
the desert by day
the desert by night
outer space
a fallen tree, dead or still growing
the wilderness next door
the wilderness in the garden
birches as Robert Frost sees them
a blend of mist, geese, sky, and water
the spirit, atmosphere, and tone of a natural place
how the earth looks to someone from outer space
a sunflower
a muddy road
the center of a cyclone
"God's own country"
running rapids
an apple tree, a cherry tree, a chinaberry tree,
    a mulberry tree
the kinds of lands the Conquistadores walked through
    (not by any means all "golden lands")
April showers
March winds
the Grand Canyon, perhaps by concentrating on its
    colors, the order of description determined by the
    change of colors with the season
the natural scenes seen by the first pilgrims in America
some natural object that suggests something else or
    someone else
"my territory"
something sight unseen
"under the sun"
a schoolwalk in the mountains, slippery with rain
a part of (or something on) the Mississippi as Mark Twain
    saw it
the landscape as seen from a descending parachute
a mountaintop as seen from it
a mountaintop as seen from the ground
a branch of madder
the "roof of the world"
a pre-dawn morning
"down-under" skies
fire on the water
a lonely mesa
a watering hole
a Peruvian landscape
a sunset on the river
a natural bridge
a dust storm

a windstorm
a place named Windy
a sun-pounding day
the call of the Rocky Mountains
the lure of the sea
treacherous waters
a path off the trodden path
signs and seasons
the sun or moon as a rider of the sky
the beginning of the world
the world as split open and seen from the inside
shadowy, mysterious trails
an approaching storm
a rainbow of flowers
dandelion season
walking in the rain
a road *not* taken
catching the dawn
catching a falling star
"my woods"
a scene just before, during, or after the Flood
a Virginia scene as Captain John Smith would have
    seen it
bringing the country to the city
the little picture in nature
the big picture in nature
a winter wonderland
redwood trees
infinity as evidenced in nature
color and light in nature
a snow in May
coming to life in the spring
sand castles
riding in mist
an early snow/a late snow
a tropical storm
a sun day
a smiling sky
winds that don't let up
tides
the "your land" part of "This Land is Your Land"
the ending of the day
a catwalk over a rockwall canyon, over thundering
    water
an idyllic setting that conveys a certain mood
a setting with the title of a famous book (such as
    How Green Was My Valley)
the quality of a natural setting by way of some
    aspect of it
unexplored territory that is terrrifying
the outdoors taken inside

the earth as "a little island of Creation amid the circumambient Void"

vegetation growing through the cracks of an abandoned house

Iguassu Falls (bigger than Niagara Falls)

Where the Sidewalk Ends (name of children's book)

pleasure gardens

country roads

the view from a hilltop overlooking a great city

an artificial environment that intrudes on a natural setting

magnificent treasures or scenery available to the beachcomber

the same scene today contrasted with that seen by another writer years ago

snow in the forest (as if you are there in it)

a natural world "charged with the grandeur of God" (G.M. Hopkins)

a honeycomb (as seen scientifically and then as seen non-scientifically)

some natural object as for someone who has never seen one (say, a tree or a certain kind of cloud)

"the Pleiades in a silver row"

a natural setting *beyond* the commercial description of it

a natural setting as seen by a microscopic eye

the indifference of nature

an everyday occurrence in nature

Where the Wild Things Are (name of children's book)

a small island in a huge, rough sea

Creature Life

Describe:

the biggest snake

spiders vying for attention by swinging from their threads

cockroaches scurrying for cover

a home where the buffalo roam

butterflies/fireflies by the thousands

mosquitoes in Paradise

circus animals

an ant with a grain of sugar

an animal that eats humans

a fox seeing a movement in the grass

a cattle roundup

stunt-flying birds

wild mustangs

animals fleeing from the enemy (man or beast)

a "kitten on the keys"

a "super horse"

the flight of an eagle

weightless birds resting on reeds

a homeless, hungry dog

Texas or Alaska mosquitoes

guard dogs on the roofs of palatial homes

a snapshot of a beloved pet

insects seeking sanctuary from humans

a praying mantis praying

flamingos in flight

a whale leaping into the air

a bird colony

a civilization of insects in one room

the path of a turtle across the road

an endangered species

a walking fish

animals in battle to the death

animals fleeing from a fire

a Yellowstone bear hunting food

a dog that is the subject of a Beware-of-the-Dog sign

a rat-infested, many-familied jungle hut

an animal (or an animal scene) in a medieval bestiary

the tiger as an image of awesomeness

a household dominated by pet cats or dogs

a civilized, almost-human, animal

gerbils jockeying for position in a revolving, circular cage

the blue dolphins such as in the book, *Island of the Blue Dolphins*

the lamb as an image of innocence

the kestrel hawk (the windhover) as an image of something that does the difficult with great ease

a school of animals—that is, a place where animals are educated

Human Beings, Individuals

Describe someone:

who does as he/she pleases

who tells you more than you want to know about one subject or another

who is "chicken" about one thing or another

who delights in disorder

who wants a tourist to take his/her picture

who is homesick

who is superior to others but does not try to show it

who has an inferiority complex

who epitomizes dignity

whose fate is a far less happy one than predicted

who works just to be busy

who hates anyone who does not love him/her

who is a good-natured egotist

who is too hot, or too cold, to handle

who has, in character, many opposing parts

who is an authority about something or someone he/she has no interest in or liking for

who is a seeker

who has a second flowering

who opposes something without understanding it

who writes up the national psychological and vocational examinations

who is a "living legend"

who is oracle, sage, and know-it-all

who is the ultimate fan

who is left speechless

who has a short fuse

who "says little, thinks less, and does nothing at all" (quotation from George Farquhar)

who is trying to look sober but is not

who delights in order

who would rather give up life than material possessions

who has a mad impulse

who is a pragmatist

who is lonely

who is at a loss for words

who behaves like a deranged and frightened Ichabod Crane

who loves rings

who has only one idea, and that one a wrong one

who is a pebble on the beach, one of the crowd

who is in spirited conversation with himself/herself

who is a compulsive taker of notes

who tries to appeal to everyone

whose identity is revealed only at the end of your description

who is shrewd

who is one of those who will "inherit the earth"

who always says, "Let's get serious."

who is a saver or collector

who practices small economies such as string-saving

who is an unofficial psychoanalyst

who is expert at avoiding serious commitment

who has to settle for a second choice

who is just learning self-respect

who is on a soap box

who is "worth watching"

who is like his/her pet

who is in love with love

who has an unusual habit

who has an unusual interest

who is free again

who has gambling fever

who looks ignorant

who looks intelligent

who looks wealthy

who looks poor

who looks tragic

who looks self-pitying

who cuts into line

who rages at God whenever something goes wrong (such as bad weather)

who is an actor without an audience

who has too little to do

who behaves characteristically

who is like Bartleby, a fictional character who says only, "I would prefer not to."

who is a "roads" scholar, a tramp

who is always "the one in charge"

who daily "goes ape" over someone or something new

who sings while at work

who is always first with the worst

who is shaped by experience

who is "crazy like a fox"

who is a pied piper

who is poetry in black

who succeeds exceptionally well in something he/she does not seem suited for

who has no enemies

who has no friends

who is a "city-slicker" in the country

who behaves spontaneously

who is a quick study, a superb mimic

who suffers from the effects of someone else's trying to break a bad habit

who is in heart but not in sight

who likes to dance

who is all business

who is dressed up to scare

who knows how to answer the question "How lazy can you get?"

who learns everything without help

who has no middle name

who *is* a middle name

who has only initials as a name

who is a name-dropper

who came very young to the throne (actual or symbolic throne) and had to come of age quickly in order to deal with the world

who is without vices

who is without a single virtue

who appears, but is not, intelligent

who appears, but is not, ignorant

who is an advocate

who monopolizes conversations

who is one of a kind

who is his own man/her own woman

who is misguidedly chauvinistic or zealous

who has a force or energy born of terror

who is like his/her residence

who is undeservedly famous

who is undeservedly infamous

who is brave in spite of an obstacle to bravery

who is a freelancer at something

who, though in an official capacity, corrects you on the facts you give about yourself

who is tight-lipped

who is a "wonder of wonders"

who is "programmed"

who is ageless

who is self-consciously middle-aged

who is a toastmaster

who is a wayfaring stranger

who is poetry in motion

whose behavior is controlled by conditioning

who is responsible for having changed your life

who is a hermit in the city

who is outlandish

who is crazy as a loon

who is a great impostor

who tries to stay on a diet

who tries to give up smoking

who tries to give up drinking

who characteristically over-reacts

who is right off the comic page

whose main weakness is _____

who is an angel

who has escaped from prison

who is a high-roller

who is flaky

who runs the wrong way

who is seeking the unattainable

who is too dangerously busy

who coaches football but doesn't know what a football is

who is "strange"

who is a born leader

who is a born follower

who is in a shaky position

who is prematurely old

who is cute (or "cutesy")

who is, though grown, a baby

who is "Nature's darling" (Thomas Gray's reference to Shakespeare)

who is godlike

who is a "good person"

who has the gift of gab

who never confesses to losing an argument

who has "coffee nerves"

who has "nicotine fits"

who delivers jeremiads

who is just plain dumb

who is spoiled by success

whose name and personality match exactly

who is like a chameleon in personality

who is describing himself/herself only by what he/she sees in a mirror

who is a caricature

who is discouraged because of having suffered in a natural disaster

who, even if not known, ought to be Man/Woman of the Year

who is confused by the world but not worried about it

who is utterly without opinion or substance

who has a face and manner of authority

who wears "the smile of God"

who is a modern Sphinx

who has absolute confidence

who can see though blind

who is coming to terms with the fact of death

who is a double for someone else

who is an "All-American" type

who has islands inside

who is so obsessed by TV as to have a pocket TV

who is tied up in knots

who is used up or burnt-out

who is blissfully unaware

who is in austerity

who is a scapegoat

who is "square" or "straight-arrow"

who is egotistical

who has an immense talent in hiding

who is eccentric

who is a good judge, though without experience

who is a picture-straightener

who is a perfectionist

who is in need of special attention

who is "always around"

who is "never around"

who is a high-climber

who is just now finding a voice

who never gives in

who delivers tedious speeches or sermons

who is "asleep at the switch"

who is a "wolf in the fold"

who is an outsider or a pariah

who is a master solicitor of funds

who is utterly imperturbable

who is easily perturbed

who has a name that sometimes causes accidental humor

who is hopeful of catching a fish

who is hopeful of finding the right job

who has insurmountable scruples

who is in prison for political reasons

who is exhausted almost to the point of death

who has noble qualities

who is a non-heroic figure

who can be characterized by speech mannerisms

who has a voice "like a great bell swinging in a dome"
(quotation from James Elroy Fletcher)

who is an esoteric scholar

who is a member or a joiner

who has (in the words of John Ford) "shaked hands
with time."

who is nameless

who dares/who "dares not" do something

who is capable of inspiring confidence

who is exotic

who is a saint

who loves the stage (as observer, or as performer)

who has many kinds of deep troubles

who is a lover of the country

who is an audience of one

who speaks to one person as if to an audience

a relative or a close acquaintance

someone as the god(dess) of something

a pickpocket in action

the child in you

a friendly president of a small country

someone you love to hate

someone with a "singing face" (quotation by John
Fletcher)

a child in the White House

a teacher with only a sixth-grade education

someone trying to sleep when it is impossible to sleep

a reluctant Santa Claus

someone who expresses an opinion without thinking

a great person known to you

a lunatic employer

someone surviving the winter

someone with laughter like a bellows action

someone who is uncommonly shy . . . who laughs, for
example, with great embarrassment at just about
anything

someone surviving a great public embarrassment

someone who is ostracized

someone who is too conscious of his/her best profile

someone before and after

someone hard to catch, hard to conquer

an uninvited guest

someone picking cotton ("snapping") with the energy
of a very young person

someone who is lovable and loving

someone who is unorthodox

someone throwing a tantrum

someone who is an authority on a wide range of *obscure*
subjects: for example, darbies, hieroglyphs, praying
mantises

a first-time Broadway playwright awaiting first reviews

someone who is a "clear-cut choice"

someone who has the lowdown on someone

someone who has retained elegance and charm

the president as through the eyes of a child

what *your* inferiority complex is like

the child in someone

an heir/heiress

someone climbing a lamp post during a celebration

the unknown soldier/the unknown citizen

a bouncer

an angel in the _____

a broken individual

your interview with a famous person

someone in the moment before death

a veteran

someone who is self-consciously kind

a night security guard at work

someone who would like to harm you

someone watching something intently

an IRS official as seen by a reluctant taxpayer

a reluctant taxpayer as seen by an IRS official

the thing in you that others admire

someone who is unknowingly self-revealing

someone surviving the loss of the savings of a lifetime

someone surviving the failure of an important
examination

someone rushing to catch a bus

someone suddenly realizing he/she is late

someone reacting to an unfunny joke

someone reacting to a speech

someone suddenly remembering something

yourself as you were at one time

someone, such as a small child, who can get dirty where
no dirt is

a lazy-lipped person

someone with a vigorously recurring (but seldom
lasting) spiritual regeneration

someone who walks hundreds of miles to prove love to
the one waiting at the destination

someone in despair

"someone I ought to know better"

an old man/woman in school

someone who "wrote the book" on _____

the top-sergeant, still more active than the recruits
after more than thirty years of military service

someone who has weathered *everything*

an underdog who likes the role of underdog

someone real or fictional who is a slumbering giant
awakening

someone who is made up of many different parts, all
of which are funny

an unusual child whom you met on a trip

someone so as to prove or disprove the following:
   "No one can read the comment behind an expression."

a petty bureaucrat

a painting—say, "The Blue Boy" or the "Mona Lisa"
   —come to life

Queen Mab as described by Shakespeare

Queen Cleopatra as described by Shakespeare

a person who uses ceremonial language for any occasion

Hagar as a living type

Senator Sam Ervin

Ali as an actor in real life

Thomas Jefferson at home

Calvin Coolidge

a once-maligned person who is lauded now

a once-lauded person who is maligned now

a globe-trotter

a person described as by William Faulkner

a thinker/dreamer

someone who is fascinated with the ordinary

a shallow person/a dull person

someone with a long comic history invented by you

someone who has beaten the odds

a once-famous Western star who is still "riding high"

someone who was right there where it happened at
   the time it happened

yourself as others see you

someone who is politely, coolly efficient

someone who is shy only because of being too proud
   to risk being made a fool of

any famous modern person at birth

yourself as in the first moment of your birth

Harry Truman

Senator Daniel Webster

Nastase, the "bad boy" of tennis

Kay Kyser

Mephistopheles as a living type

someone made hesitant or too cautious by a bad
   experience

Human Beings, Groups

Describe:

autograph hunters

soldiers in the face of battle

evangelical preachers

people celebrating a special occasion

a bread line

dj's

strangers, wanderers, gypsies, wayfarers, other transients

drive-in-movie groups

a bullfight crowd

an enthusiastic opera crowd

everybody trying to get into the act

a society in boots

sightseers

a seance

a teenage dance

a political convention

a private club

a metropolitan bus station in Latin America

people who carry their pasts around

people who leave their pasts behind

the early Vikings

any group of remote primitive people still living

rabid fans

prisoners

people who help others

old people living in a hellish existence

the sunglasses crowd

the whole neighborhood

people who visit

fireside chats

an all-week party

people in droves

people at Bingo Night

the rat race

an SRO crowd

the activity at a fair booth

a POW camp in the United States

an old-fashioned talent show

people who make every day a holiday

muscle flexers

a private party

an amusement-park crowd

a sidewalk sale/a fire sale/a rummage sale

a citizen protest

people who are profiles of courage

people who are profiles of excellence

a hog-calling contest

downtown Saturday Night

Londoners during wartime attack

the gates of heaven

much ado about something

much ado about nothing

a slave auction

the end of the world

a hometown celebration

a wedding party

the delivery room of a hospital

people in the streets of Paris during the French
   Revolution

people in the streets of Paris celebrating the end of
     World War II
inhabitants incongruous with the contents of their
     living room
the crowds on Fifth Avenue or some other famous
     New York City thoroughfare
baseball announcers
the crowded stands at the Super Bowl
pedestrians, traffic, and the resulting confusion when
     all try to cross a small bridge at the same time
the Bolshoi Ballet
a TV show in England dedicated to the weirdos
a fast-draw championship
the ceremony at the beginning of a bullfight
the gates of hell
the Gold Rush
a sleepy tourist town in the country of "Costa Bella,"
     a banana republic
"*our* crowd"
Bohemians at home
shantytown living
the delivery room of a department store
the luggage-recovery section of a major airline
Palm Springs life
an athletic team for which nothing goes right
a bilingual theater troupe
"just a big mess," anywhere
people in silly season
kids on the last day of school
hell of the subways
the family pew
the firemen's/policemen's ball
the Rainbow family
a crowded beach
a sleepy village and its inhabitants
people saying goodbye
a "country on the brink of democracy"—riots, troops
     in the streets, etc.
the scene-behind-the-scenes for a certain film production
a big publishing house
a fair/a stock show
a night club crowd as *you* see the people
"unpersons"
missing persons

Places and Things

Describe:

a private museum
table scraps; leftovers
a worn record
a burning barn
a ghost town

the view from a train window
a hidden treasure
what was found in the unearthing
a public notice
a historical document
stained-glass windows
a particular painting
a "speakeasy" of Prohibition times
a roadside attraction
coals and embers
a condemned hotel
a lost-and-found office
Main Street
hand-me-downs
a bowl of cherries
a double-dip ice-cream cone
a little black box
a piece of ancient metalwork
a tapestry
an ancient book
a certain architectural style
a wrecking yard; a car dump
a deserted stage
a square inch of ground
a ferry boat carrying twice the number of passengers
     it should
a place named Easy Street
a theater in the thickets
strange constructions
a ship passing by
something close-up and then faraway
the scene from the inside
the scene as viewed by the Statue of Liberty
the scene from a lighthouse
something that is sterile in appearance
the lure of old almanacs and diaries
a book by its cover
a black book/an address book
the sense of being there where it happened—at
     Dunkirk, say, or at Hastings
a certain poster
a mystical setting, using mystical terms
what's in a purse
what's in a pirate's sea chest
what's inside a home on the Aegean Islands/Aran Islands
a pawn shop
a single-room schoolhouse
a sandbox
Air Force One
something without revealing what it is until the end
a quiet place

an old-age home
a child's home
a telegraph station in the 20s
the dust under the carpet
a medal
a gimmick
Las Vegas/Paris/New York
cereal-box surprises
The Book of _____
a work and hobby bench
something Byzantine-like
a world inside a doorknob
signs of the times—road signs, etc.
something from Eliot's *The Wasteland*
a golf course that has some unusual hazard
a *pentimento* painting
what you see from the top of _____
the land passing by as you stand on a ship
the scene from the balcony
the scene from the back seat
the scene from the top of the Washington Monument
something that is dingy
Hell as if it were a certain city
antique items in a house abandoned years ago
the last book
an image from yesterday
"a lamp unto our path"
the oldest city in the United States
Bath, England, as it was in the Middle Ages or before
a glass menagerie
a mystical setting, using concrete terms
a watch on the Rhine
what's in a medicine cabinet
a bell
a dilapidated boat
an unusual house
the local bookstore
a single-room house
a soldier's home
a door (one of the hardest things to describe: because it is so common)
a map
a Viking ship
a shelter
something hard to find in a large city
an oilspill
a synthetic future
the scene after a picnic
a huge foreign city
a new product
a small efficiency apartment

a greasy-spoon cafe
the town dump
the last place on earth
old haunts

Senses, Intangibles

Describe:
early-morning sounds
electronic music
Sunday smells
smell of hops, etc.
smell of wet wool blankets—the smell of black wool
what you feel when you look into outer space
the effect of a certain piece of music on *all* the senses
a certain musical style
the joy of playing a certain musical instrument
rich little touches in a book, movie, musical performance
"a shining artistic achievement"
serenity
time/timelessness/eternity
God
the "indescribable" by using unusual terms
the sixth sense
"more than a feeling"
"winter dreams"
the ever-changing flame of a candle
a dream house as a house that one has dreams in
an impulse or a compulsion
a situation that admits of ambiguity or ambivalence
upside-down looks
the misery of _____
"sublime noise" (E.M. Forster's allusion to Beethoven's *Fifth Symphony*)
occasional silence
something "full of sound and fury"
a kind of hush
a "dirge without music" (Millay's term)
a pompous speech
being alone in outer space
Fourth of July spent in a foreign country
Christmas away from home
the oceans of visions and sounds of thought in the waking and the sleeping mind
God as if through, or by, one of His creations
"shaking the spheres of the universe"
"the splendour of a sudden thought" (quotation from Robert Browning)
feeling free (in the sense of *unrestrained*)
a dream within a dream
the dreamlike quality of something

the intangible quality of something
deja vu
a dream come true before the dream is dreamed
a bizarre bazaar
the action and thought of an instant's time
it (*or* It)
a magic dream dance
a gesture which has deep meaning
a state of mind
"not with a bang but a whimper" (Eliot)
where _____ begins
listening in nature
the joy of solitude (as recorded in a diary)

Actions/Miscellaneous

Describe:

a favorite kind of job
a bureaucratic operation
sticking together
mending a fence with someone
beaming signals
something comforting
the turn of the screw

a sneak preview
camera eye
the difficulty of sharing a secret
the interesting people you meet at _____
going home
undoing a great damage
recapturing prisoners
biting the dust
a parachute jump
a discus, javelin, or weight throw
the maneuvers of a non-glamorous position in football
flying off the handle
blocking the view
the last straw
hunting in a trash pile
_____'s Day
the center of attention
what there is to do in _____
a compromising position to be in
so as to answer the question, "What have we got here?"
on-the-job training
swapping roles
diversionary tactics
a showdown

COMPARISON/CONTRAST

What Comparison/Contrast Is

As a literary device, comparing and contrasting things to gain a heightened impression of them is as old as . . . well, as old as Homer. Here, abridged, is how James Joyce parodies one of those Homeric similes: "Clinging to the sides of the noble bark, they linked their shining forms as doth the cunning wheelwright when he fashions about the heart of his wheel the equidistant rays whereof each one is sister to another. . . .Even so did they come and set them, those willing nymphs, the undying sisters." Joyce would have us spoke our literary wheels with a craftsman's care and cunning. One of the handiest and most natural ways to do that is to compare two things that are somehow alike, or contrast one thing with something dissimilar in a certain telling way. Recall how the contrasting tones of a black-and-white photograph can cast a face into such compelling relief, or how Vemeer's colors beat so vividly in the dim lowland sun. That much and more comparison/contrast can do for language.

How to Write Comparison/Contrast

One way to use this device effectively is to make sure the things compared or contrasted fit. We might, for example, compare a redwood tree with a rosebush, but it probably would not gain us much beyond a laugh. If it is the skyscraping stature of the redwood we are after, we might compare it instead with the stalk that Jack climbed into the land of giants. The redwoods would be at home there.

Or we could compare a young Latin American guerrilla, son or daughter of a peasant, with an American college student who goes to a business school, not because he or she feels impelled to work in business, or is even much interested in it, but because that is where the surest money is. The comparison might lead us to a study in irony, though probably there would be little room to sow much seed in the common ground between the two young people. This is possibly the place, then, where *contrast* might be more effective. Let us say that we contrast that same guerrilla with a young person from the revolutionary's own country: child of a wealthy landowner, graduate student in economics at the University of Chicago. The two threads of such a contrast could weave the social fabric of a nation and pattern the history of our time. One secret of comparison/contrast, then, is harmony.

Locating Subjects for Comparison/Contrast

Beyond the specific listings in this chapter, this book as a whole might itself become a study in comparison/contrast. It could certainly be readily used that way. Compare, for example, the chapter on description with the chapter on research-and-report writing. Contrast creative writing with process writing, and so on. All the approaches to writing discussed here are spokes for the wheelwright's craft, all are sisters.

People

shepherds/cattle drivers
actors off-screen/actors on-screen
a historical figure in two different periods of
    his/her life
cliff dwellers/New York apartment dwellers
fellow travelers/tourists traveling together
the nomad/the homebody
a certain person/the same person transformed
country person/city person
a "nobody"/a "somebody"
the first mate on an 1850 ship/the CPO on a 1940 ship
religious leaders of different religions over centuries
the adolescent as doer/the adult as doer
historian/dramatist
model of society/the average person
the just/the unjust
a gullible person/a stupid person
San Martín/Bolivar
the same person in and out of uniform
one person in two roles
generals/privates
an alcoholic/a drinker
innocent today/guilty tomorrow
the right person/the wrong person
two all-time best players
person poor/same person rich
married person/single person
generation one/generation two
changing people
the mathematical mind/the mechanical mind
European Latins/American Latins
the needy/the greedy
congress/parliament
a past star now not a star
upper crust/lower crust
born to lose/born to win
fictional TV figure on camera/fictional TV figure
    off camera
a friend now an enemy
an enemy now a friend
the temperaments of _____ and _____
two faces of _____
mixed/matched
blue-collar workers/white-collar workers
child like an adult/adult like a child
the Stoic/the Epicurean
the lyricist/the composer
a real person/the depiction of him/her on television
Billy Budd/Claggart
revivalist/used-car salesman

a "tiger"/a "pussycat"
one rebel/people rising up as one
how one sees oneself/how others see one
the scholar/the untutored
the private logic of _____ and _____
different parts in same person ("Two souls, sadly, are
    in my breast."—Goethe.)
two gamesters, each playing in the usual role of the
    other
one kind of thinker/another kind of thinker
the actor/the role the actor plays
the uniformed person/the person out of uniform
amateur/professional
attorney/doctor
person on offense/person on defense
original/imitation
seeming free/not being free
ordinary person/uncommon person
the same person, tough and tender
citizen/non-citizen
the best/the worst
1880 students/1980 students
salesclerk/customer
hearts made of stone/hearts on fire
young college students/old college students
Einstein/Newton
compulsive reader/bookworm
pedestrian rights/driver rights
people modern and ancient in their view of the universe
folk rock singer/hard rock singer
the forever friend/the sometime friend
Benedict Arnold, before and after
the one blamed/the one who should be blamed
the powerful/the powerless
Shakespeare's Macbeth/a modern Macbeth
the young and their values/the old and their values
aristocracy/tyranny
student unrest/student rest
upstairs people/downstairs people
scientist's view of the stars/poet's view of the stars
actors as they were in their old roles/actors as they are
    now in their old roles
two major candidates for the same office
American opera stars/Italian opera stars
Eton student/Harrow student
Harvard student/Yale student
movie actor/television actor
movie actor/stage actor
ideal American/real American
oneself/old friend
oneself/young friend

the person given the credit/the person who should have gotten credit

a famous person/someone who looks like the famous person

oneself/one's conscience

companionship/friendship

a person rich/the same person poor

what I wanted/what I didn't want

Compare/contrast life in a polygamous society with that in a monogamous one.

Compare/contrast "day people"/"night people."

Compare/contrast these opposing bases of marriage: In some cultures, it is said that "you don't marry the person you love; you love the person you marry."

Compare/contrast yourself with Thoreau . . . as, for example, on the issue of imprisonment.

Compare/contrast yourself with another part of you to answer the question whether you are good company for yourself.

Compare/contrast a public figure sober with the same public figure under the influence of alcohol.

Compare/contrast little professional football players with big ones.

Compare/contrast famous people with their children.

Compare/contrast famous people with their parents.

Compare/contrast in a theme, "Anything But What I Expected."

Compare/contrast the negative views of yourself against the positive ones.

Compare/contrast one person who has two occupations.

Compare/contrast the native of a country with a tourist to that country, keeping in mind that natives are not tourists in their own country.

Compare/contrast tourists/explorers.

Compare/contrast the assassination of one president with that of another.

Compare/contrast yourself with someone like you.

Compare/contrast yourself with someone not like you.

Compare/contrast two people who are much alike in many ways.

Compare/contrast so as to show someone changing a role—Aladdin, for example, doing something for the genie.

Compare/contrast someone's bark and bite.

Compare/contrast the TV-watching habit with some other habit or obsession.

Compare/contrast the Russians and the Americans of the Diomedes Islands.

Write a comparison/contrast essay concentrating on the happiest people in the world, considered as a group such as a country.

Write a comparison/contrast essay concentrating on the moodiest people in the world, considered as a group such as a country.

Write a comparison/contrast essay concentrating on the kindest people in the world, considered as a group such as a country.

Use comparison/contrast to show that, as Cicero believed, the minds of persons are the persons themselves.

Use comparison/contrast to argue that, as Henry Fielding wrote, there is at least one fool in every marriage.

Use comparison/contrast to show that, as Sir William Hamilton believed, on earth there is nothing great but humanity; in humanity there is nothing great but mind.

Use comparison/contrast to show whether a clergyman can be an entertainer.

Use comparison/contrast to show whether a politician can be an entertainer.

Use comparison/contrast to show which counts more in football: brawn or brain.

Use comparison/contrast to show which requires more work: casual dress, or fancy dress.

Use comparison/contrast to relate the *beginnings* of the careers of Johnny Unitas and Dan Fouts, both of quarterback fame.

Use comparison/contrast to write on the subject, "If I can't have _____, I'll take _____."

Use comparison/contrast to show whether the choice at the polls is one more of comparison than of contrast.

Use comparison/contrast to show that disabled persons are more like the undisabled than different from them.

Use comparison/contrast to write of someone, unlike the average person, who would take the smallest piece of something good and give the best and largest piece to a neighbor.

Use comparison/contrast to show that in politics it is often the one who makes the next-to-the-last mistake who wins.

Use comparison/contrast to show the proof of the headline, Navajo Life Similar to That of Third World Nation.

Use comparison/contrast to show that, as William Cowper believed, God made the country and human beings made the town.

Use comparison/contrast to show how, according to Anna Barbauld, society is worse than solitude, and one human being with another is still the greatest curse.

Use comparison/contrast to show that, as Oliver Wendell Holmes argued, the world's great people have not commonly been great scholars, nor its great scholars great people.

Use comparison/contrast to show that, as William Lloyd Garrison believed, our country is the world and our citizens are all humanity.

Use comparison/contrast to show that it is reasonable

that, as Mme Cornuel believed, great people are not great to their valets.

Use comparison/contrast to show that, as Oliver Goldsmith believed, little things are great to little people.

Use comparison/contrast to relate Richard Nixon and Shakespeare's Richard II.

Use comparison/contrast to discuss the following: A political cartoon shows two people watching *Holocaust* on television. One of them asks, "How on earth could civilized people just sit back and allow all that to happen?" Ih view of the reader is a newspaper headline reading: More Soviet Jews Jailed.

Comparison/contrast topics about humanity may be drawn from the following:

"Though it be a foul great lie: Set upon it a good face" (Bishop John Bale).

"The face the index of a feeling mind" (George Crabbe).

"Ask not what your country can do for you but what you can do for your country" (John F. Kennedy).

"When students get good grades they say Look what I got; when they get bad grades they say Look what the teacher gave me" (newspaper item).

"Hanging and marriage go by Destiny" (George Farquhar).

"I describe not people, but manners; not an individual, but a species" (Henry Fielding).

"There is so much good in the worst of us,/And so much bad in the best of us,/That it hardly becomes any of us/To talk about the rest of us" (Edward Hoch).

"Registered foreign agents differ from unregistered foreign agents in two notable ways. First, they are not here ostensibly, anyway, to steal state secrets. Second, most of them are not foreign" (Jack Anderson).

"I AM in good shape," says a cartoon bum; "you should have seen me last week."

"I've had distemper and I've played mixed-doubles," says Snoopy, who would rather, he says, have distemper.

"Be careful with him: He's going to be a father" (Ronald Colman, speaking of his dog, in a movie).

"There are two kinds of people here in Washington," says a cartoon—"those who know what's going on . . . and the rest of us."

"It is impossible to enjoy idling thoroughly unless one has plenty of work to do" (Jerome Jerome).

"Is a team better off resting for a week or staying sharp under game conditions?" an AP article asks regarding the NBA playoffs.

"Americans, of course, hold no monopoly on producing memoirs. The practice of celebrating the great leader's life by putting pen to paper (or hiring a ghost) dates back at least to Caesar's 'Commentaries' " (re Nixon's memoirs, newspaper article dated May 29, 1977).

"It is easier to love humanity as a whole than to love one's neighbor" (Eric Hoffer).

"The real American is all right; it is the ideal American who is all wrong" (G. K. Chesterton).

"Queen Anne was one of the smallest people ever set in a great place" (Walter Bagehot).

"Full many a flower is born to blush unseen" (Thomas Gray).

"The people have little intelligence, the great no heart. If I had to choose I should have no hesitation in choosing the people" (Bruyer).

"They're only truly great who are truly good" (George Chapman).

"If youth knew; if age could" (Henri Estienne).

"Mediocrity knows nothing higher than itself, but talent instantly recognizes genius" (Sherlock Holmes).

"To be nameless in worthy deeds exceeds an infamous history" (Sir Thomas Browne).

"All the world over, I will back the masses against the classes" (William Gladstone).

"Because you are a great lord, you believe yourself to be a great genius! . . . You took the trouble to be born, but no more" (Pierre Beaumarchais).

"The living need charity more than the dead" (George Arnold).

"I have been a stranger in a strange land" (Bible).

"Know most of the rooms of your country before you cross its threshold" (Thomas Fuller).

"It is the province of knowledge to speak and it is the privilege of wisdom to listen" (Oliver Wendell Holmes).

"Good families are generally worse than any others" (Anthony Hope).

"The love of liberty is the love of others; the love of power is the love of ourselves" (William Hazlitt).

"The most fluent talkers or most plausible reasoners are not always the justest thinkers" (William Hazlitt).

"Some are weather-wise, some are otherwise" (Benjamin Franklin).

"It has been said that although God cannot alter the past, historians can; it is perhaps because they can be useful to Him in this respect that He tolerates their existence" (Samuel Butler).

Human Conditions

dark days/happy days
choice between two roads
nearsighted, farsighted
style, comfort
discrimination/absence of discrimination
fasting/feasting
orthodox/unorthodox
two kinds of birth
mule lag/jet lag
dating in high school/dating in college
lazing/relaxing

new look, new life

derring-do/derring-don't

discrimination of one kind/another kind of discrimination

private things/public things

felt obligation/momentary pleasure

dating in England/dating in the U.S.

two kinds of death

mind/heart

mind/brain

honor/fame

delusion vs. reality in sports and sportsmanship

lean years/fat years

habit/disposition

God's gifts/human dreams

progress/improvement

apartment living/dormitory living

Compare/contrast two procedures at birth.

Compare/contrast the views two different cultures have of death.

Compare/contrast an incipient society with an extinct one.

Write a comparison/contrast essay showing whether the noblest thoughts and actions came from the people who lived in the desert or from those who lived in fertile areas.

Write a comparison/contrast essay on the subject, Things Gone Good.

Write a comparison/contrast essay showing that some things are common to us all.

Write a comparison/contrast essay on the theme, You're Only Old Once.

Use comparison/contrast to show what the world would be like if millions of people exactly like you had controlled the progress over these past six million years.

Use comparison/contrast to show what it is besides courage that is opposed to cowardice.

Use comparison/contrast to show that blindness is, as has been said, "another way of seeing."

Show by comparison/contrast someone in nature and out of nature.

Show by comparison/contrast that, like a person, a neighborhood (or a class, or a country) has its own personality.

Show by comparison/contrast whether the big things, or the little ones, shape our lives.

Hagar says that the whole idea is to catch the enemy off guard; just around the mountain bend is an Italian troop whose leader is saying the same. Compare/contrast behavior of opposing groups.

Consider from the point of view of both individuals and the United States government whether we know as much how to solve our own problems as those of others.

Snuffy Smith is behind jail bars; his son Tater is behind the bars of his crib. Show by comparison/contrast how two different people or two different groups of people have their own kinds of jail bars.

Compare/contrast on the basis of the title of the popular self-help psychology book, *I'm OK You're OK.*

Compare/contrast on the basis of the title of an article in *International Wildlife*, "Animals Are Only Human."

Comparison/contrast topics about the human condition may be drawn from the following:

"Love is consistent, hate is random" (proverb).

"Chains are worse than bayonets" (Douglas Jerrold).

"Dying is more terrible than death" (Henry Fielding).

"Cheer up, the worst is yet to come" (Philander Johnson).

"Old families last not three oaks" (proverb).

"I'm saddest when I sing" (Thomas Bayly).

"Into each life a little sun must fall" (L. E. Sissman).

"Just remember one thing, son, " says a cartoon father: "I know a lot more about being young than you know about being old."

"The act is all, the reputation for it nothing" (Goethe).

"Religion's in the heart, not in the knees" (Douglas Jerrold).

"Why is it the political party out of office is the only one that knows how to run the government?" asks the "small society" cartoon.

Science and Nature

drought/oasis

thorn/flower

alligator/crocodile

plowing under/harvesting

toads/frogs

animals as humans/humans as animals

the mallard/the _____

green/ripe

the coral snake/the snake confused with it

life on earth/life in outer space

hot ice/hot wind

animal intelligence/human intelligence

two animals in intelligence

hands/hands

simple foods/fancy foods

natural gas/lignite

good things of spring/not-so-good things of spring

anthropology/sociology

domestic plant/wild plant

two sides of nature

snowflake/snowflake

hay fever/asthma
honey/bee
coldblooded/warmblooded
feet/feet
someone set in nature/nature itself
insect/another of its genera

A French actress says that in speaking English you use fewer facial muscles than in speaking French. Compare/contrast the subject by your own investigation.

Use comparison/contrast to show that nature has a way of keeping up its own beauty and humanity has not found a way to improve on natural beauty.

Using comparison/contrast, discuss the observation by an astronomer, Dr. Benjamin M. Zuckerman, that human beings from earth are the smartest in our galaxy.

Distinguish between nothing on one hand and, on the other, coming into existence where there had not been anything before.

Compare/contrast the chestnut tree, the tulip, or the comet described by the scientist on the one hand, the non-scientific philosopher or poet on the other.

Compare/contrast someone who has an affiliation with nature with someone who does not. Show, for example, how the former can merge naturally with the landscape while the latter seems out of place.

Language

and/but
old saying before/old saying now
plain and simple/plain and fancy
oasis/watering hole
inhibition/restraint
known/renown
good conversation/ordinary conversation
thought/expression of thought
libel/slander
objectivity/subjectivity
left as political term/*right* as political term
table/mesa
bureaucratic language/clarity
introvert/extrovert
major speech/minor speech
re-creation/recreation
The Mother Tongue/The Father Tongue
possibility/probability
the timeless West Wind/the timeless song
something before being translated/something after being translated
Scriptures in one language/Scriptures in another
pessimism/optimism
grammar cognition/ability to write

denotation/connotation
what is said/how it is said
turned on by/turned off by
speaking as people write/writing as people speak
induction/deduction
legalese/"legal-ease" (to quote *Time* magazine on improved legal terms)
English in England/English in America

Write a comparison/contrast essay in which you delineate a conventional truth using unconventional terms and ideas.

Use comparison/contrast to make a dull idea sound interesting.

Use comparison/contrast to make an interesting idea sound dull.

Translate Biblical figures of speech into modern "cool" speech.

Compare/contrast a headline and an article under its heading that does not match it in content.

Use comparison/contrast to write of a new way to be dull.

Use comparison/contrast to write of a new way to be interesting.

Compare/contrast changing ideas of what "well-balanced" means to a psychoanalyst, a cook, or a coach.

Use comparison/contrast to show what William Hazlitt meant in saying of Charles Lamb the essayist: "His sayings are like . . . letters; all the pith is in the postscript."

Education, Knowledge

wisdom/knowledge
curiosity/inquisitiveness
conventional teaching/Montessori teaching
natural law/divine law
thinking/letting the mind wander
a philosopher/a non-philosopher
book learning/practical learning
homework time/television time
objectivity/subjectivity
philosophy/religion
modern math/regular math
learning/teaching
a book/another book of the same kind
early focus children's books/modern focus
opinion/belief
mental energy expended over a long time/mental energy expended over a short time
logic/common sense
college graduates then/college graduates now
knowledge in one situation/knowledge in another
what is right/what is taught to be right

Compare/contrast the popular idea of what an educated person is with your own idea.

Compare/contrast a narrow professional area and a wide professional area: generalist teaching vs. specialist teaching, for example.

Use comparison/contrast to show whether today's child can read better than today's adult.

When do you think best, when you are sitting or when you are on the move?

Use comparison/contrast to show that, as Mortimer Adler has declared, a book has a body and a soul.

Comparison/contrast topics about education and knowledge may be drawn from the following:

"Where ignorance is bliss, 'Tis folly to be wise" (Thomas Gray).

"What I don't know isn't knowledge" (Henry Beeching).

"A book may be amusing with numerous errors, or it may be very dull without a single absurdity" (Oliver Goldsmith).

"Knowing things is being them" (Ortega y Gasset).

"As light is greater than darkness so wisdom is greater than folly" (Bible).

"To learn something new, take the path you took yesterday" (proverb).

"Poetry is something more philosophical and of graver import than history" (Aristotle).

Places, Perspectives

up close/far away
clockwise/counterclockwise
over/under
NYC 1950/NYC 1982
Chinese communism/Russian communism
city alive with activity/large city deserted
detente/_____
coming/going
state/country
big town and little town identified by the same map
one placement office/another placement office
space/the opposite of space
booing/hissing
military bureaucracy/civilian bureaucracy
same solution, different results
outskirts/inskirts
here/elsewhere
two different places of burial
forever-home/sometime-home
Alberta/Texas
southern pampas vs. northern pampas of Argentina
up against the ceiling/up against the wall
ups/downs
ins/outs

Chicago/New York City
light penalty for something/heavy penalty for same thing
Western ways/Eastern ways
my house/your house
top half, bottom half, each making the other possible
two sides of a certain hotel, house, or town

Use comparison/contrast to show disparity in what free speech is and what it is not.

Use comparison/contrast to answer the question: What is happening in this very moment in other parts of the world?

Use comparison/contrast to show that sometimes forward and backward, up and down, are all the same.

Use comparison/contrast to discuss a truth as large as an astral body but rarely seen.

Write a comparison/contrast essay on a change of feeling, place, or situation.

Compare/contrast something other than in the conventional or popular way.

Write a comparison/contrast essay to show that nothing stays the same.

Write a comparison/contrast essay to show that (to translate from a French expression) the more things change, the more they remain the same.

Compare/contrast cloak-and-dagger conceptions with real espionage.

Write a comparison/contrast essay that answers the question, What is happening in this very moment in different parts of outer space?

Which is better, a harmless lie or a hurtful truth?

Compare/contrast the changing perspectives about scholarship, law, or machinery.

What happened to you at this same moment in another time—or, what will happen in some future time at this same moment?

Use comparison/contrast to show a person before and after he or she is out of sight.

Compare/contrast the same kinds of orchards in different parts of the country.

Use comparison/contrast to show how the political definition of the "Solid South" has changed over the years.

Compare/contrast two kinds of strategies for a campaign, a game, or a speech.

Use comparison/contrast to show the way a certain building dominates other buildings around it, even if the other buildings happen to be taller.

Use comparison/contrast to show how things change by the addition of some foreign substance. How, for example, would a virgin forest change by the addition of a priceless jar set into its midst?

How does the average citizen of Western Europe live differently from the average citizen of the United States?

Compare/contrast a situation in the "Land where the light is darkness" (Bible).

Comparison/contrast topics about places and perspectives may be drawn from the following:

"We are as near to heaven by sea as by land!" said Sir Humphrey Gilbert.

"Were Niagara but a cataract of sand, would you travel your thousand miles to see it?" wrote Herman Melville.

"Where Christ erecteth His church, the devil in the same churchyard will have his chapel" (George Bancroft).

"They are ill discoverers that think there is no land, when they can see nothing but sea" (Sir Francis Bacon).

"It's always morning somewhere" (Richard Horne).

Economy, Trade

Compare/contrast ways of spending and mis-spending.

Write a comparison/contrast essay about old money vs. new money.

Write a comparison/contrast essay that distinguishes the dollar from the confederate note.

Compare/contrast money in one part of the country with money in another part.

Compare/contrast the dollar in the United States with the dollar in some other part of the world.

Compare/contrast two cars for gas economy.

Use comparison/contrast to distinguish between economy and economics.

Use comparison/contrast to distinguish between wet goods and dry goods.

Use comparison/contrast to distinguish between old values of farmland and modern values of farmland.

Compare/contrast the manufacture of something—candles or soap, for example—then and now.

What was a Stone-Age financial depression like?

Discuss by comparison/contrast: "In this economy average is below average," says a cartoon.

Measurement

Compare/contrast the Arabic number system and the Roman number system.

Compare/contrast metric measurement with another principal kind of measurement.

Compare/contrast simplicity and precision.

Compare/contrast equal rights and equal wrongs.

Compare/contrast two things usually thought to be equally good.

Compare/contrast two things usually thought to be equally bad.

Compare/contrast something thought to be possible by one, impossible by another.

Compare/contrast statistics that mislead and "honest" statistics.

Compare/contrast compliment and insult.

Write a comparison/contrast on the subject, Going to Great Widths.

Write a comparison/contrast on the subject, Little but Important.

Write a comparison/contrast on a topic suggested by one of the following: the wrong emphasis; every other inch; overlapping.

Compare/contrast the degree of frightfulness in the realistic and the supernatural.

Comparison/contrast topics about measurement may be drawn from the following:

"A minute's success pays the failure of years" (Robert Browning).

"Between good sense and good taste there is the same difference as between cause and effect" (Bruyere).

"It is the nature of all greatness not to be exact" (Edmund Burke).

Art and Entertainment

this movie/that movie

television comedy/society

circus from inside/circus from outside

wrestler as actor/actor as actor

two great architectural types

art criticism by self/art criticism by others

hit song/non-hit

movie acting/stage acting

American movie controversiality vs. foreign movie controversiality

background vs. foreground in painting or photography

humor/black humor

movie acting/TV acting

British TV ads and frankness/American TV ads and frankness

British TV as it is/British TV as it is thought to be

fictional character/same character given your name

Past and Present

old city, new city side by side

electric typewriter/manual typewriter

old demands, old conditions/new demands, new conditions

the generation gap then and now

British Bobbies then/British Bobbies now

old commandments/new commandments

old views of divorce/new views of divorce

military training then and now

past danger/present danger

the same fable, old and new

old and new dentistry

old-time religion/modern religion

the world then/the world now

ancient adobe-brick/modern adobe-brick

Compare/contrast a situation in which something old has been added.

Compare/contrast what wildcatting was like in Alaska thirty years ago with what it is like today.

How did the treatment of children during the Middle Ages differ from that of today?

Compare/contrast Prohibition laws with today's marijuana laws.

Write a comparison/contrast essay to show that things are not that simple anymore.

Write a comparison/contrast essay to show that things (or, the times) are better, or worse, than they were before.

Compare/contrast old and new soap-opera scripts.

Compare/contrast a situation in which the modern and the primitive co-exist comfortably side by side.

Compare/contrast the before-and-after of an old picture or an old event.

Compare/contrast Greenwich Village before and after.

Compare/contrast a situation in which something new has been added.

Compare/contrast politics (or some part of it such as language) before and after Watergate.

Compare/contrast the medieval ways and the modern times in a modern city.

Compare/contrast the medieval ways and the modern ways in a medieval city.

A Hagar cartoon shows that a battering ram was the medieval equivalent of today's doorbell. Using comparison/contrast, draw other relationships of a humorous kind between medieval times and present ways.

"Let my people go," says Egypt to Israel, in a cartoon. How does the saying contrast with its usual application?

See the opening paragraphs of Conrad's *Heart of Darkness*, where there is a description of England as it must have looked to the conquering Romans. Compare/contrast Conrad's description with a description of the modern scene of the same area (even if it is your own description rather than one you find).

Seeing the movie *Soldier Blue*, someone said: "They sure were violent back in those days." Point up by comparison/contrast the unintended irony in the statement.

Use comparison/contrast to discuss this quotation from Eisenhower: "Things are more like the way they are now than they ever were before."

Use comparison/contrast to discuss the import of the following: "In old time we had treen chalices and golden priests, but now we have treen priests and golden chalices" (Bishop John Jewel, 16th century).

Use comparison/contrast to discuss the following: "It's tough being retired," says "the small society" cartoon. "You live in the past at today's prices."

Analogy

a person's life/a book

river/mother

Henry VIII/Ozymandias

a person/a city

a person/a parade

professional football/nuclear warfare

an adult's home/a castle

eternity/moment

life/party

life/TV show

life/football game

camera/eye

writing/composing

New York City street/battlefield

backpacker/kangaroo

music/language

animals/United States presidents

marriage/driving

novice police officers conducting traffic/novice conductors conducting musicians

a building/an ocean liner

a blind date/a surprise package

a child's room/a kingdom

a mind/a kingdom

an island/_____

eating with chopsticks/_____

mind/eye

beer foam/bomb

the Irish Sea/_____

fame/river

fullness of life of a human being/ant with sugar grain

dance hall/church

home/country

architecture/nature

Analogical subjects may be drawn from the following:

"Every drop of the Thames is liquid history."—John Burns.

Luther said that people stay busy as a factor making things to worship.

"Slavery is a weed that grows in every soil."—Edmund Burke.

In our destinies are we more like buses, free to move in any direction, or like trains, fixed in our tracks?

Understanding that, in one way or another, all the world reads, compare and contrast that kind of reading with writing.

"Superstition is the religion of feeble minds."—Edmund Burke.

"Love is like linen often changed, the sweeter."—Phineas Fletcher.

"Reasons are not like garments, the worse for wearing." —Robert Devereux.

"Money speaks sense in a language all nations understand."—Aphra Behn.

"Every tear from every eye/Becomes a babe in Eternity." —William Blake.

"A good book is the purest essence of a human soul." —Thomas Carlyle.

"Justice is truth in action."—Disraeli.

"It was my tongue, not my soul, that cursed." —Euripides.

"The leaves of life keep falling one by one."—Edward Fitzgerald, translation of a line in *Omar Khayyam.*

"The tree is known by his fruit."—Bible.

"Bad laws are the worst sort of tyranny."—Edmund Burke.

"The tongue has no bones," F. L. Lucas said, "but it can break millions of the bones of human beings."

"For how agree the kettle and the earthen pot together?"' —Bible.

Show by analogy what sense some nonsense can make.

"Inflation is the neutron bomb of economics. It destroys everything in your bank account while leaving the figures intact."—*The Houston Chronicle.*

PROCESS

What Process Writing Is

Process writing generally tells the reader how to do something, or how something is done, by proceeding one step at a time. This procedure may be used in anything from a recipe to a repair manual to the complexities of a political movement. Process writing might best be understood as a particularly disciplined form of exposition.

How to Write Process

As implied above, the central feature of process writing is that it proceeds from one point to another in whatever sequential order (logical, chronological, physical, mechanical, and so forth) the subject demands. The key to effective process writing is shaped to an orderly selection and presentation of the material. In that sense this form is usually more stringent than some of the other forms might be. The writer who breaks the sequence and disrupts the procedure, risks jumbling the process and confusing the reader. But this does not mean we should use the key to process writing to lock the form in its tomb. Robust verbs and trenchant nouns will keep it alive.

This type of writing is especially useful for technical subjects. Here is a simple example from an article in the *Scientific American*. It has to do with a device that allowed Galileo to use his telescope as a measuring instrument: "There was a circular grid with a diameter of ten centimeters and a spacing between rulings of about two millimeters. The grid had a pin through its center by which it was attached to a rod ending in a ring that fitted snugly around the tube of the telescope. When Galileo looked through the telescope with his right eye, he looked with his left eye at the grid and optically superposed Jupiter on the central pin. The grid was then rotated to align a horizontal ruling with the plane of the satellites. . . ."

Locating Subjects for Process Writing

Process writing can become an important part of any other type of writing, including the most creative variety. Its relevance to the other parts of this book will be evident. But concentrating on some of the subjects listed in this chapter—ranging, as they do, from "how gravity works" to "how football drafts work"—and moving them step-by-step through a rigorous, concrete, and clear explanation would be a helpful exercise for anyone who wants to write anything at all. Process writing is that fundamental. The student who does it well will then be well into the process of learning the writer's craft.

Food and Drink

closeting fine wines
making earth bread
using the microwave
butchering a rabbit
choosing a wine
making frankfurters
baking in a sand pit
making *arroz con pollo*
preparing fried rice
preparing refried beans
charcoaling
broiling
making candy
making tacos
making a combination pizza
making a flour tortilla
making a cake
making a spicy spaghetti sauce
presenting a recipe on TV
shopping for food in a foreign country
eating with chopsticks

Writing

using footnotes
writing to _____
writing argumentation
writing more simply
using the pronoun "you"
writing pompously
writing an F paper
organizing a paper
saying nothing in many words
taking notes
proofreading
achieving clarity, brevity, correctness, simplicity, or thoroughness in writing
educating oneself to know areas one is writing in
writing a job application
writing a good composition
writing a short story
writing an introduction to a composition
thinking creatively
imposing "discipline on the dream" (Irving Wallace quotation, referring to following up with an inspiration)
sound writing or sound-writing
marking compositions
keeping verb-tense consistency

registering in writing a complaint about writing
getting down to the agony of writing

Education, Learning Processes

using the *Reader's Guide to Periodical Literature*
looking up words in a dictionary
predicting success or failure
taking an advanced course
answering a question
wasting time effectively
meditating
using mnemonic devices
figuring by the Chisanbop method
failing at something new
teaching a language by a special method
saving private schools
getting or losing accreditation
communicating when you don't know the language
bringing out whatever talents you have
reading or teaching Braille
getting preliminary experience or education
learning how to read everything
reading in context
learning argumentation by practicing it or reading it
reading for the blind
learning without taking notes
using the library card catalog
finding out information
explaining
pushing for excellence
using newspapers in the classroom
prescribing knowledge for oneself
reading a totem pole
teaching a first reading lesson
reading sign language
choosing children's books
reading a map
learning how to ask the right question(s)
planning a degree
reading body language
doing mental arithmetic
learning to like _____
telling an illustrative story
being more observant
making drudgery exciting
learning how to put things off as long as possible
how children play
how parents can start a school of their own
how Alexander the Great was tutored

how television has changed learning

how well-to-do children were educated in England during the 14th century

how a university is organized

how to be understood

how to solve discipline problems in elementary school and high school

how Montessori works

how playthings help the child grow

how a blind artist works

how to use trial and error

how some of the hardest lessons are the simplest to learn

how a child (grows, learns, loves)

how we learn what we have already known

how to skim-read by skipping judiciously

how to experiment by the scientific method

how conversation can be taught

History

How were duties relegated in medieval abbeys and monasteries?

How are war criminals tracked down?

How did a certain Latin American country put down a coup?

How is the past recaptured?

How can one "know" by going to history?

How did Thomas Paine write?—that is, by what persuasive method?

How did Napoleon plan the invasion of Russia?

How did King George see the American Revolution?

How did Elizabeth I improve her navy?

What was it like to _____?

How can the forebears of a certain famous contemporary be traced?

How does a country surrender to another country in time of war?

How is wartime neutrality maintained?

How did DeValera rise to power in Ireland?

How did the draft system (conscription) come about? How did it first operate? What changes were made in the operation in subsequent years?

How is genealogical research conducted?

How is the coast defended?

How are votes from certain groups courted?

Nature

how the earth is weighed

how gravity works

how nature resolves overloading

how (in Bacon's terms) we command Nature by obeying her

how ants construct colonies

how African termites build castles

how spiders spin webs (according to kinds of webs)

how the trout goes upstream

how the wasp traps the spider

how the cuckoo nests its eggs

how to curb erosion

how mountains are made

how antlers are used

how fireflies can be used

how a bloodhound can follow a trail

how to conserve natural resources

how coffee is produced

how the weather is predicted

how infinity is measured

how *flora* and *fauna* are protected

how fruits and vegetables are inoculated

how insects, birds, reptiles, etc., live on their internal food reserves

how snails battle

how ants battle

how spontaneous combustion works

how creatures are protected from extinction

how the Grand Canyon was formed

Human-and-Creature Processes

how wildlife is photographed

how lakes are stocked with fish

how to fish in salt water

how to breed fish

how to tame a rabbit

how to crossbreed _____

how whale blubber was sliced in the 19th century (as explained in *Moby Dick*)

how to get rid of troublesome birds or animals without killing them

how to train an animal for a television commercial

how to talk with animals

how to milk by hand

how to rid a dog of fleas

how to breed a mule

how to shoe a horse

how to fish the old way

how to find the angle for angling

how to bird-watch

how to fish for halibut

how to humanely get rid of gophers from under the house

how to share your backyard with wildlife

Games, Sports, Outdoor Activities

how to judge a contest
how to use a sail bike
how to perform a certain figure in ice-skating
how to get lost in the wilderness
how to hunt for underwater treasure
how to hand-load a _____
how to load a blunderbuss
how to hit the bull's-eye
how to prepare for a hunting trip
how to find the right tent
how to equip for a backpacking trip
how to practice falconry
how to trail-ride
how to pick a winner
how to warm up
how to win hands down
how an umpire/referee calls
how to keep long-distance bicycling from becoming
    painful
how to set the stage for females in formerly "male"
    sports
how football drafts work
how to maneuver a sailboat
how to stay fit for _____
how to shoot baskets the way a professional does
how to steal bases
how to teach a certain move or certain stroke in tennis
how to get the hang of hang gliding
how to run the 100-meter dash
how to use strategy to win the race
how to use strategy rather than brute force in _____
how to win at badminton
how to set up the football wishbone; how it works
how to challenge an umpire without being thrown out of
    the game
how to perform a certain kind of high jump
how to juggle
how to ride a unicycle
how to make a certain wrestling hold or movement
how to swim a certain stroke
how the middle-aged should train for a marathon
how to take an early-morning constitutional
how to get up again after falling down (in skating or
    skiing)
how to lift weights the wrong way
how to perform a certain judo hold or movement
how to throw a bowling ball
how to cut corners in skiing
how to deep-sea dive
how to ribbon-rope in a rodeo

how to fly a kite
how to mountain-climb
how to perform a certain water-skiing maneuver
how to become a roller-baller
how to skateboard
how to teach the blind to ski
how to ski cross-country
how not to win at _____
how to be disqualified in _____
how plays are called from the bench
how to shoot a certain kind of gun
how to set up a certain chess strategy
how a jockey is responsible for the success of his/her
    mount
how to hike with the family
how to walk a certain style
how to run a certain style
how to perform certain calisthenics
how a guide can help you in hiking

Religion

how someone is excommunicated
how someone is exorcised
how one becomes canonized
how to enter the priesthood/ministry
how the Pope is chosen

Airplanes, Air Travel

how flight accidents are investigated
how the first balloon was flown
how to survive a plane crash
how to skywrite
how to fly over the Alps (or Andes)
how to plant-spray
how to fly—as a bird, passenger, or pilot
how to barnstorm
how to land a plane where there is no airport
how a fire-engine airplane works

Cars, Road Travel

how to drive defensively
how to get a driver's license revoked
how to catch a car thief
how to put a car together from scrap
how used-car dealers lie to prospective customers
how to take a driver's test
how to control the car pollution
how recalls of cars are made
how to care for a car
how to get more miles out of a gallon of gas

Travel, Travel Preparation

how to pack a suitcase
how to call from one country to another
how to get a visa
how to get a passport
how to hitch a ride
how not to hitch a ride
how British soldiers crossed the Darien Gap of
    lower Panama
how to get medical help abroad
how to make reservations
how to travel heavy
how to travel light
how to protect your luggage—from loss, from theft
how to ride a bus or train in a foreign country
how to visit _____
how to travel in Europe
how to travel with a family
how to order a meal where you don't know the language
how to get paid for travel

Telephones, Telephoning

how telephone cables work
how to trace a telephone call
how toll-free numbers work
how a telephone operator works

Grooming

how to use dental floss the right way
how to find the right clothes for the right time
how to cut hair
how to groom without using cosmetics
how to choose the right soap, shampoo, or other toilet
    article

Sleep/Sleep Processes

how to go to sleep by not trying to go to sleep
how to wake up a little bit at a time
how to learn the fine art of napping

Entertaining, Social Arrangements

how to run a restaurant
how to eat at _____
how to play bartender
how to be a bore at a party
how to have fun at a party
how to arrange a surprise party

how to plan a party for teens
how to arrange a wedding

Safety

how to put out an electrical fire
how to put out an oven fire
how to put out a grease fire
how to react if mugged
how to prevent electrocution
how to use a flak jacket
how to protect yourself in a natural disaster
how to have a contingency drill—for fire, attack,
    disaster, etc.
how to protect yourself on the street
how to guard against poison plants
how to prevent childhood accidents or diseases
how to make _____ safe
how to cycle safely
how to keep camp life safe

Medicine, Physiology, Health

how to bear children at home
how the human embryo develops
how to trace the cause of a certain sickness
how Lincoln's medical history could be researched to
    speculate on his health during his second term
how to pick the sex of the unborn
how to avoid unnecessary health-care and hospital
    expenses
how a bypass operation is performed
how to implant a lens
how to deal with jet lag
how doctors and nurses proceed in an operating room
how to treat oxygen lack
how to eliminate most deaths from _____
how scientists proved the link between smoking and
    cancer
how to save your teeth
how to find out what's wrong when the doctors won't
    tell you
how a liver machine has helped liver patients survive
how asthma is treated
how the root-canal is treated
how a face-lift is performed
how cryosurgery works
how polio was conquered
how a certain vaccine was discovered or developed
how breast cancer is detected and treated
how alcoholism is treated
how to test for allergies

how to treat bee stings or insect bites
how to cure acne
how to deal with frostbite
how to stop hiccups
how the pacemaker works
how to use the Heimlich Maneuver to save a choking
    victim
how to sunbathe safely
how the heart works
how the brain works
how to improve your sleep
how to correct a lazy eye
how to test for twins in the last trimester of pregnancy
how to determine whether TV "pain relievers" are
    dependable
how an MD makes a medical prognosis
how to cure infection of _____
how to fight against infection
how an organ is transplanted
how to still butterflies in the stomach
how to treat snakebite
how to perform a certain operation
how to take blood pressures
how to treat poisoning from poison plants
how to give artificial respiration
how midwifery works
how to read temperatures

Constructions, Constructing

how the Pyramids were constructed
how sewage systems worked during the Victorian era in
    England
how dams are built
how windmills are constructed; how they work
how oil pipelines are constructed under water
how to make adobe bricks
how to make impossible architecture possible
how to lay the groundwork for a house
how to build a crib
how not to design an auditorium
how to build a sandbox
how to make a _____ chair
how to make a _____ table
how to misconstruct a house
how to shingle a roof
how to construct a model inside a bottle
how to perform a certain kind of carpentry
how to make a porcelain figure
how to build a dugout
how bridges are constructed for strength

Repairing, Cleaning, Inspecting

how to inspect a restaurant for cleanliness
how to window-clean tall buildings
how to clean up a town
how to repair potholes
how to mow a lawn or trim hedges
how to wash clothes the old way
how to clean a chimney without putting a chicken
    inside and letting it fly out
how to paint a _____
how to refinish a _____
how to repair an icebox
how to repair a heater
how to repair a bicycle brake
how to service a _____ tape recorder

Art, Handicrafts, Domestic Arts

how early Disney animation worked
how to animate
how to foreshorten in drawing
how to contour-draw
how an art work is preserved or repaired
how an art work is examined for authenticity
how to make a collograph print
how to draw with a pencil
how to draw with charcoal
how to engrave
how to turn scraps into decor
how to hang wallpaper
how to decorate a room
how to quilt
how to sew by a pattern
how to make clothes better and more cheaply than you
    can buy them
how to display your collectibles
how computer art works
how to do macramé
how to do batik
how to adjust a television set for _____

Plant Life

how fruits and vegetables are picked, processed, packed,
    and sent to the consumer
how to plant grass
how to clone redwood trees
how to plan a spring garden
how a seed grows
how to protect trees
how to get an orchard on the way

how to control the growth of grass
how to start off with house plants
how to cut a blue spruce for a Christmas tree
how to develop a green thumb

Money, Business, Saving, Theft, Economics

how smuggling is done
how to prevent hotel thefts
how to make out an income-tax return
how to read a drug prescription and save money
how to take measures against shoplifting
how bill collectors draw blood
how to collect on your insurance
how to save money
how travel agencies work for remuneration
how the IRS catches tax-evaders
how to plan an economical trip
how the phone company is defrauded out of payment
    for long-distance calls
how customers rip-off the electric-power companies
how customers are ripped-off by public utilities
    companies
how the economy of a foreign country can be
    undermined
how to spot counterfeits
how to keep from being reckless with credit cards
how Thoreau lived on next to nothing
how to live off the wilderness
how money is spent by charity organizations
how to live simply
how to boost tourism in _____
how to collect unemployment
how to conserve energy in the home
how to sell _____
how to have a garage sale
how land fraud can be exposed
how to buy public land
how to end unemployment
how teenagers can pay their own college costs
how millionaires spend their money
how money is "laundered"
how old money is discarded at mints
how the teller operation works jointly
how to retire in peace
how to exchange money at borders
how countries that have disasters are helped financially
how dividends are determined and distributed
how a hospital is administered
how to take care of your bills while you are away
how to live within a salary or an allowance
how charity organizations work

how money is printed at the mint
how returned goods are paid for in the long run
how to get rich without marrying someone wealthy
how a stock exchange works
how grocers deal with differences in shopping habits
how to sell your own book
how to hunt for a bargain
how to buy at an auction
how a Dutch auction works
how the realtor works after an agreement has been
    reached to buy or sell a home
how to trade foreign money without getting taken
how ancient traders did without money
how to lose a job through incompetence

Film, Film Media, Photography

how to use a camera in soft light
how to keep a camera clean
how to take a picture with an old camera
how to pick out an inexpensive manual camera
how photographs get across the world in a short time
how to develop films privately
how Hollywood screen extras work
how television ads are pre-screened for bloopers
how to set up a television translator
how to keep a television translator going
how the laugh machine on television works
how an actor or actress plays a double role (or more)
    in the same take
how old filmmakers showed the passing of time
how modern filmmakers show the passing of time
how old filmmakers moved from one scene to the next
how modern filmmakers move from one scene to the
    next
how a television producer works
how a movie producer works

Language, Information, Communication

how to break a code
how the Chinese calendar works
how the Aztec calendar works
how computers answer mail
how to interview
how to behave in an interview
how libraries have changed since early days
how to outline
how to understand computer language (such as COBOL)
how Hitler used propaganda
how the AP works
how the news is slanted
how the English language developed from its beginnings

how words change meanings
how Webster worked on his dictionary
how slang becomes acceptable
how to break the language barrier
how to set up a debate among presidential candidates
how to debate on TV as a presidential candidate

Mechanical and Chemical Processes

how to test a driver for alcohol
how to program a computer
how a rotary engine works
how to bug an office
how the new invention works
how an oil well works
how _____ can be kept afloat (or aloft)
how to build a better mousetrap
how the Hughes toolbit worked
how a ticker-tape works
how to use earphones
how the first liquid-fuel rocket worked
how to desalt water
how to purify water
how to control a certain kind of pollution
how outer-space germs are controlled
how moonshine can be a cheap, efficient substitute for
    gas in automobiles
how sugar is refined
how copper is refined
how sulfur is mined
how coal was first mined
how strip mining is done
how waste can be converted for use
how mummies were mummified

Psychology, Emotions, Social Actions

how to take on the "epidemic of failure"
how to change jobs
how to prepare for job-hunting
how to check on one's own honesty
how to come to a family decision
how to bring out the best in _____
how phenomenology works
how the secretary handles the public
how to live with a two-year-old child
how children blow off steam
how to keep a poker face
how to abduct someone's mind
how the person under psychoanalysis can get along
    while the doctor is away
how to kick a habit

how to live with a Waterloo
how to heal emotional wounds
how to control the violence that exists in us all
how to make the mind wander effectively
how to relax correctly
how to go beyond your endurance
how to end post-meal hunger
how to pull your own strings
how to get your first job
how your first job went
how to change thought-focus and thus remove worry
how the human machine works
how to release a friend from an obligation
how to fire a friend
how to make employees work better
how to check the voice for lies
how the public is sometimes "emotionally blackmailed"
    by public servants
how to get along with an older (or a younger) brother or
    sister
how to get away from someone
how to deprogram a person
how to psych-out your opponent
how to recover from an emotional blow
how to get back on the road to confidence
how to get over feelings of guilt
how to avoid a scene (or other unpleasantness)
how the child changes from age 12 to age 13
how thought worked before the evolution of language

Law

how to profit from complaining legally
how to sue a city
how to protect yourself legally from the landlord
how the taxpayer can legally revolt
how to make a class-action suit
how to settle an account without trouble
how to shop at an antique store
how to unload a lemon legally
how border officials crack down on narcotics
how border officials can better crack down on narcotics
how aliens are registered in the United States
how to get a permit for _____
how whistle-blowers are protected from their superiors
how the small-claims court works
how the teletype gets instant results for the police
how a court decision can be challenged
how to read fingerprints
how a lawman is trained
how to make up a legal petition
how lawyers are protected from those they help convict

how to let thieves know you are not at home
how to help police in their work
how to proceed if arrested
how those who await trial are treated
how judges perform their duties
how to make a citizen arrest
how to prevent a certain kind of crime

Government, Politics

how a census works
how to end the bureaucracy
how the government protects historical settings
how a town council can bring about the resignation of a city official
how to lobby
how to burrow into office when another party comes into power
how to run a national campaign
how computers pick the winners
how political pressure is applied
how a government agent penetrated the intelligence panel of a foreign power
how sabotage was committed
how sabotage was discovered
how a press secretary operates
how a Senate Committee investigates
how a President is elected
how the Supreme Court operates
how to ratify an amendment
how Russia chooses its top government official
how the American political process works
how the "loyal opposition" is supposed to exercise its duty
how majority rule operates
how national polls are taken
how to locate someone in a bureaucracy whose shins you can kick

Miscellaneous Processes

how fakery works in _____
how to find the killer
how to speak out against abuses
how someone becomes thoroughly Americanized
how to infiltrate a narcotics ring
how the first American tools were made
how to scare a reader or a moviegoer
how not to be scared behind the wheel
how accuracy is checked for world record claims
how to select the right stereo
how to identify babies with their mothers

how the U.S. Geological Survey researches its map information
how (or of what) cattle die
how to get tickets for a television show
how the Muppets work
how to live primitively
how to behave like a _____
how to conduct a _____ contest
how to collect valuable stamps, coins, etc.
how applications for employment are verified for such things as education and work experience
how to expose a rip-off or a con job
how to acquire free land in Canada
how to see backwards into time
how misprinted money is handled
how to put things together in order to understand their relationships to one another
how to take _____ apart
how to meld or blend _____
how to shave comfortably
how to drift
how to break a routine
how to thwart
how language adds words
how to stop _____
how to keep going in _____
how to get started
how to perform a certain monumental task
how _____ (money, a ship, a grade) was raised (or can be raised)
how to stalk the wild _____
how _____ works
how to revamp _____
how to learn the ropes
how to make a practice run at _____
how to get along better with your _____
how to observe something
how to collect art
how to learn the music scales
how a fire station works
how an advertising agency works
how to arrive at the same result by opposing means
how to paint what is not there
how to read music by sight
how to undo something
how a major hotel operates
how forest lookouts work
how an airport control tower works
how the metric system was arrived at
how the system other than the metric system was arrived at
how to make a miniature _____

how to audition
how hunger works
how to make a guitar
how to get from here to there
how sweat glands work
how to make radio contact
how to get rid of a cold
how to take an injection without falling apart

how to recharge a _____ (something other than a battery)
how missing heirs and heiresses are located
how to get a job as a forest ranger
how thinking can be made into a hobby
how art can enrich life
how imposters fake their qualifications
how old paper money is disposed of
how Pulitzer Prize winners are chosen

NARRATIVE

What Narrative Writing Is

A narrative tells a story or gives an account of what happened. It is certainly one of the oldest forms of communication. One thinks of Homer again, of drawings in prehistoric caves, of ancient oral traditions—all of them narratives. Life itself is a narrative, a history, a story (Latin, *historia*). Would anyone's deepest heart not recognize and respond to that truth? It seems fair to say that people everywhere have always looked with pleasure and a certain awe towards the one who could tell that story well.

How to Write Narrative

It is no accident that this chapter on narrative follows the section on process writing. There is no question here about how those two spokes in the rhetorical wheel relate. The "and then and then and then" of the narrative is close indeed to the sequential advance from point to point of the process writing. A similar attempt at precision and clarity should be made, but at the same time the narrative form demands that the writer be allowed more freedom. A narrative line may often be kept straight and strong by twining process techniques through the core of it. But here the rope must be allowed to fray, to soak up the smells, the colors, the taste, and the touch of circumstance. A good storyteller knows how to draw a long bow, the better to whistle the arrow dead to the heart of the matter.

Of course there are other, far more radical, narrative liberties. Many contemporary novelists delight in them. Most beginning writers, however, would probably do well to learn how to spin a straight yarn before they tangle it, web intricate plots, and risk getting the narrative confounded.

Locating Narrative Subjects

Everyone has a story to tell, and it would not hurt anything to shame students who insist that their lives are so dull that they cannot write interesting narratives. There are stories everywhere, in just about anything, and this book offers no exception to that commonplace. Still, it is hoped that the subjects in this chapter will goad memories, spark imaginations, in a special way. Close attention could as well be paid to the chapters on creative writing, critical writing, and description. There is surely something here that should arouse any student to relive, in writing, an experience (even if the "experience" originates in the imagination) that ought to be shared.

Domestic, Personal, and Autobiographical Narratives

the coming fury
stuck with it
the most important
unopposed
the addict
revealing for the first time
secretest thoughts
five minutes more
fluffs and bloopers
talking it over
punning around
good news
seeking independence
seeking identity
in the back of my mind
not being predictable
gaining a son/daughter
ready for a new start
orphanage days
blowing dust
on the brink
a special sound
winter love
at the wrong hour
a personal message
being spurred on
skipping class to do something else
job for the inexperienced
to a peak
determined to be
the oldest of many
one example, repeated to extinction
plunder
unexplained act
convertible car
not ready yet
hot shot
Saturday afternoons
do or die, now or never
in command
the first day
the last day
cramping my style
all at one time
advancing steadily
making up for lost time
your turn now
best offer
old catalogs

a secret vote
names on the masthead
bird in the hand
the last one
rising again
under dire circumstances
private word
working off a debt, moral or financial
a real-life supernatural happening
disappearing
closing a chapter
leaving someone for the first time
on the take
topping this or that
a place of honor
with this ring
howdy
spiders and snakes
doubtful deeds
even now
vacancy/no vacancy
a week ago
the target of threats
being bitter/not being bitter
first visit
trouble with the manager
claiming to be someone else
home to stay
flirting
dirty work
more than the usual
hearing/listening
last-gasp effort
fleeing
precognition
short-changing
fighting the doldrums
signing on, signing off
self-righteousness
principals and principles
just looking on
making up
gone but not forgotten
some changes or else
show of good faith
look who's talking
two for the money
critic's choice
critic's corner
alone in _____
when all is said and done

rediscoveries
frivolity
delay of check
winning a prize
under fire
nothing the same
doing it best
still up in the air
in distress
laughing/not laughing
being ready
World's Greatest
The Last Season
for seven years
after school
hooray
separate ways
every step of the way
learning to adapt
sometime laughter
feeling no pressure, feeling no pain
yuletide
getting the gold star
hoax
somewhere between
a significant aside
in conquest of others
playing second fiddle
to go, or to eat here
teacher outdone by pupil
blankety-blank
something I can't put behind me
small change
getting down
four-poster history
everybody and nobody
one sour note
anything for a drink of water
the measure of _____
Going Hollywood
Going, Going, Gone
May/December marriage
broken promise(s)
not alone
sounds and silence
sounds of silence
end of a song
taking consolation
a roaring wind
once over lightly
clearing the air

walking a dog
shielding someone
following someone
the awful truth
the last laugh
a country kitchen
favorite child
little joys—being lovingly nuzzled by a horse, for
    example, or playing in the fields, or eating a nickel
    pickle
nearing the finish
(wo)man hours
in disgrace
asking for money/the car/permission
parental bond with child/children
a charmed life
story behind the story
not being afraid
they all laughed
discovery of my father/mother/sister/brother
revitalizing spirits
breathing new life
friendship with _____
homemaking
in traditional dress
reflecting once more
nursing
separating
one step closer
wake-up call
music
making merry
an instant's attention
watching with amazement and alarm
day or night
being a complete person
earning a living in an unusual way
eating your heart out
a serious mistake made in childhood
a shot in the arm
a funny kind of _____
variety
not over yet
footing the bill
nerves on edge
a time and a place
shut away
honey of a deal
last-minute change
bridal shower
a stillness

many happy returns
hanging on
a word from home
a family affair
in the midst of life
a day spent with a living legend
hot time in the old town tonight
being an army brat
winning in a bargain or barter with a shrewd individual
only recently
sleeping on it
breaking loose
entering the mainstream
spending time
first results
too much of a good thing
early responsibility
seeing the family only rarely
greatest personal success
caring
face to face
coming full circle
clearing the tracks
lesson from the expert(s)
talking and thinking backwards to remember the past
dogfight
a voice of time/Time
going through it like everyone else
being predictable
reminding of someone or something forgotten
much ado about nothing
almost alike
unmoving minute hand
bearing the pain
taking the cake
footing it
someone following
Long Time A-Waiting for Tomorrow
freedom personified in action
favorite spot
one day at a time
reunion/uniting old pals
the last word(s)
honest mistake(s)
a really worthy accomplishment, and all mine
when I fall in love/when I feel in love
climbing through the window late at night
losing the key(s)
second helping
puppy love/love of puppies
on becoming 18

on becoming 21
making ends meet
where the heart is
green, green grass of home
defender of the _____
the day of reckoning
Ozark living
stage fright
bad moment
an instant's lapse of attention
humbling experience
supplicating
the beautiful today (meaning, to Henry Miller, the today
    that is beautiful)
asterisk for special attention
the simple made hard

Dreams, Fantasies, Make-Believe

free as the birds
setting the world on fire
Bigfoot
glorifying _____
invincible
the first moments before Creation, when God, in
    Shelley's words, was "weary of vacancy"
windjammer
meeting an archetype
dreams in technicolor
magic
pantomime
nightmare(s)
till the end of time
back from heaven/hell
soapbox
the Soviet point of view
with the original Berserkers
family dream(s)
terror from the sky
out of time
dream(s)
the coming and going of dreams
rewriting history
maelstrom
supernova
living symbols and images

Sports and Their Analogies

interference
winning combination
tennis without a net

loser take all
breaking the line
landing some big ones
dust-biting fish
giving no quarter
reruns/repeats/playbacks
illegal procedure
sportsmanship
no substitute for rules
showcase talent
back seat to no one
maximum performance
two out of three
watching _____ run
the winner explaining how it was done
turkey season
glider, gliding
down the homestretch
loose ball
strategic error
making all the difference in the outcome
overbearing
fast service
rained out
gone fishing
fishing as a "contest against nature" (Steinbeck)
a big sweep
crossing swords
athletic court as symbol for size of solar system
blockbuster
house race
over-confident

Travel, Adventure

lost in the blizzard
O, Paris!
big move
and away we go
incident at a border crossing
climbing a volcano
slow, unanxious ride
meeting in _____
fugitive
muddy road
last journey
someone met on a trip
surviving a natural disaster
the first/last bus/train/plane home
on the loose
long way yet

captains courageous
going where?
having been where?
roving
long and rocky road
the beckoning of faraway places
stacked tombs and other strange things
hard traveling
bon voyage
taking chances
Pullman adventure
head-to-head combat
driving
visiting with national park workers in a foreign country
easy way back
the nomad finding a home
asking for something in a foreign tongue
fording a river
stopping by the wayside
adrift on the Amazon
drifting
foreign friendship
on a bus
strange places
born to danger
waiting all night for a ferry
going, not going
a blowing norther
already there
hard way back

Mystery

at a seance
the uninvited
incident unexplained
accident, or homicide?
no stone unturned
black cat
looking for the one that got away
investigation
mystery behind reality
at random
first discovery of the strange
sabotage
proofs
suspicion
a voice of eternity
surprises galore
portent
undiscovered country

waiting for what comes next
chasing down a stolen/missing item
strange doings
dream house (where you have dreams)
flickering lights
impending but unseen or unknown danger

Manners and Morals

out of tune
in the long run
nose for news
threat becoming actuality
folk custom
tricky going
health-food addiction
Hail!
confusing bureaucratic experience
people of leisure
keeping up with the _____
glad to be here
at home/not at home
always watching, always being watched
honor among thieves
jury of peers
threat
a lesson for all
disco
swimming upstream (metaphorically)
sitting/standing on ceremony
knowing what to do
breach of faith
laughing at/being laughed at/laughing with
curiosity-seeking
supporting locals
maneuver, strategy
spitting venom
shootings
race with the devil

polite applause
common-sense scorn, as for UFO sightings
a pledge of quality
setting an example
snubbing
covering for someone
dog-biting man
louder, please
handling being famous
follies of the wise
choosing only one

Miscellaneous Narrative Items

Write a descriptive narrative in which you re-create in the mind of the reader an understanding of some unusual experience you have had (or have heard about from someone close to you).

Write a narrative essay entitled, "Someone for All Reasons," about a person who was everyone and everything—say, a college president or a high school principal or a mayor who tended not only to administrative matters but also swept the sidewalks.

Use the example of one of these writers for a guide to your own autobiographical narrative: James Baldwin, Max Beerbohm, James Boswell, Charles Dickens, Ralph Ellison, Benjamin Franklin, James Joyce, Jack London, Herman Melville, George Orwell, Plutarch, Katherine Anne Porter, William Saroyan, Alexander Solzhenitsyn, Henry David Thoreau, Mark Twain, Thomas Wolfe, Tom Wolfe, William Wordsworth.

Write a narrative essay entitled, "If Anything Good Can Happen, It Probably Will." A possible opening could be, "To tell the truth I am sickeningly optimistic."

Use one of the following as a beginning for a narrative essay:

Without even trying, I have come face to face with the renowned.

What I planned to say and what I did say in my first public address were not remotely similar.

Draw suitable narrative topics from the section of this book on creative writing.

CLASSIFICATION/DIVISION

What Classification/Division Writing Is

The most immediate example that can be offered of this kind of writing is the book itself, which at the very least is an extended exercise in classification/division. The material of the book is classified in terms of various types of writing and then divided into more specific categories. Classification, then, is the systematic arrangement of something into classes—groups usually founded upon some common ground. Those classified groups may then be divided into their separate parts. Strictly speaking, it is virtually impossible to classify without dividing, but for rhetorical purposes it might be helpful to think of division as tending to be more distinct, more particular. We might, for example, *classify* Russia as a country of Europe, but when we *divide* it into its geographical, cultural, and ethnic parts another more complex picture is created.

How to Write Classification/Division

As with process writing, the key here is order, the systematic arrangement of our material. An essay on "types of pain," for instance, might begin with the classification of pain into its two general types, mental and physical. That general classification could then be divided into the almost innumerable kinds of mental and physical pain. Pain, physical, emotional, psychological, can range from a nagging discomfort to an agony so unbearable that the afflicted person prefers to die. It is easy to see why the kind of writing this chapter is concerned with can be, then, an effective method for exploring such a wide-ranging notion.

Locating Subjects for Classification/Division

As pointed out before, this book is a handy example of classification/division. It might be of help to browse through it to mark how thousands of diverse subjects can be classified and divided. Of course you will be looking at lists for the most part. Once classification/division is taken beyond the list format, other writing types and techniques will come along quite naturally. James Joyce, playing Virgil to our Dante, can guide us through another circle of our rhetorical wheel. We can see in the following how he makes a beggar out of Leopold Bloom by pushing definition through classification/division into description and characterization:

> Mendicancy: that of the fraudulent bankrupt with negligible assets paying 1s. 4d. in the pound, sandwichman, distributor of throwaways, nocturnal vagrant, insinuating sycophant, maimed sailor, blind stripling, superannuated bailiff's man, marfeast, lickplate, spoilsport, pickthank, eccentric public laughingstock seated on bench of public park under discarded perforated umbrella.

Taken from: <u>What Can I Write About? 7000 Topics for High School Students</u>

----by David Powell

Animal Life

unique ways of trapping
ways of taking care of animals
kinds of unwanted animals
emotional problems of animals
ways of training animals
rare animals
animal variety on Galapagos
the smartest animals
common diseases of animals
ways of standardizing fish names
the dumbest animals
parts of an animal skeleton

Intellectual, Psychological, and Emotional Perceptions and Reactions

various ways to look at _____
ways of organizing thoughts for _____
kinds of non-physical weapons
kinds of hints, innuendos, accusations
kinds of old ways to learn
ways of looking at trees
kinds of intellectual climate
kinds of emotional sieges
the dreadful, the bad, and the not-so-bad
kinds of epiphany that influence life
kinds of impressions teachers/students have on one
    another
kinds of response(s) to crises
kinds of time thieves
several ways the world reacted to _____
emotions involved in courage
kinds of logic or rationale
kinds of knowledge
kinds of perception
kinds of "erroneous zones"
ways of observing
kinds of madness
kinds of terror
kinds of symptoms of violent patients
id, ego, superego
kinds of conditions under which it is impossible to
    concentrate
kinds of ways of opening paths to reconciliation
kinds of emotional retreats
kinds of pain
kinds of psychological games
ways in which _____ is manifested
kinds of dilemmas
personality types

kinds of ignorance
new ways to learn
kinds of temptations
kinds of taste(s)
kinds of thinking
kinds of moral courage
moods according to season
moods according to days of the week
moods according to certain incidents
kinds of ways of looking at something (using "Thirteen
    Ways of Looking at a Blackbird," by Wallace Stevens,
    as a guide)

Law

kinds of law(s)
kinds of legal professionals
kinds of legal fields
kinds of procedure by the defense
kinds of indemnity
kinds of homicide
kinds of appeals
extortion, kidnapping, blackmail distinctions
kinds of strange laws
degrees of felony
kinds of procedure by the prosecution
kinds of jeopardy
kinds of evidence
kinds of British legal professionals (barrister, solicitor,
    and so forth)
kinds of legal terms from Old English law (such as
    byrthynsak, the theft of as much as could be carried
    on the back)
kinds of summons
kinds of legal courts
kinds of waivers
kinds of fraud

Human-Made Structures

kinds of structures by human beings
kinds of living quarters
kinds of architecture of modern times
kinds of toys that are harmful
kinds of harmless toys
kinds of canoes/boats
kinds of adobe bricks
kinds of cheap hotels
kinds of specialized hotels
kinds of ancient architecture
kinds of bridges
kinds of clocks

kinds of train cars
kinds of furniture
kinds of television antennas
kinds of beds that cause trouble in sleeping
kinds of towers
kinds of monuments
sophisticated bicycles

Natural Phenomena

kinds of drinking water
kinds of snow
kinds of mind-affecting plants of Mexico
Alexander Pope's classification, "The Great Chain of
    Being"
kinds of sunsets/sunrises
kinds of colors
kinds of gray seasons
kinds of Medieval classification of the elements
kinds of clouds
kinds of storms
kinds of sounds
kinds of order among natural things

Arts, Entertainment, Showcases

kinds of crime novels
tragicomedy, comedy, tragedy
Ken Maynard, Bob Steele, Hopalong Cassidy,
    Tex Ritter, etc.
convict writers
super heroines, real or fictional
ways horror movies scare or surprise us
kinds of popular music
kinds of interpretation of art
kinds of literary schools
kinds of style in art
kinds of style in literature
kinds of criticism of art
kinds of art critics
different new books
"Faces and Places of Good Ole Country Music" (title of
    an article)
types of TV detectives
looking for the best juke box
kinds of parades
Judy Garland's various talents
kinds of pop art
kinds of literary expression (surrealism, expressionism,
    impressionism, etc.)
kinds of oral entertainment
kinds of art not requiring special training

kinds of art
Jerome Kern, Cole Porter, Irving Berlin
kinds of composers
kinds of musicians
kinds of talk shows
different audiences as seen by actors
kinds of fictional works
kinds of poetry
kinds of literature
kinds of schools of art
kinds of views of humanity in art

Social Concerns

organization of the (local, state, federal) government
kinds of social status
kinds of city problems
divisions of Harlem
kinds of slavery (not just physical slavery)
things common to criminal acts in certain areas
kinds of social units
national parks and monuments
new trends in dating
the boring 1950s, rebellious 1960s, selfish 1970s, etc.
kinds of things seen as status symbols in third-world
    countries
kinds of mail service considered by country
charities that overspend on advertising
kinds of war
kinds of governments
societies in the Orwell novel, *1984*
kinds of views of what obscenity, profanity, and
    pornography are

Religion, Myth

the astrological groups
kinds of sinners/sins
ways the Medievals viewed the sins
ways the ancient Greeks honored their gods
types and sub-types of religion
major world religions
kinds of Judaism
various kinds of belief
kinds of Medieval clergy
kinds of prayer
kinds of diabolism
kinds of Protestantism
kinds of opportunities to "get religion"
kinds of Eastern religions
Indian ways of worship
kinds of devils (or, names of kinds of devils)

kinds of geographical divisions in the United States by religion

kinds of supernatural figures in folklore

kinds of Western religion

Communication and Rhetoric

kinds of sentences

internal monologue, monologue, dialogue

kinds of insults

kinds of announcements for occasions

kinds of election conclusions: humorous reactions

kinds of books

kinds of questions that children ask

kinds of language you use depending on your audience

kinds of television ads

kinds of titles for royalty

kinds of ways the secretary's responsibilities change with the employer

kinds of laughter

kinds of flasher cards, bumper stickers, etc.

kinds of charisma

kinds of language within a single language

kinds of narrative

ways of addressing an audience

kinds of compliments

methods of news analysis

different levels of expression

kinds of funny things children say

kinds of roles you play depending on your audience

ways in which language is imperfect

kinds of rhetoric common to rebels of all time

ways of communicating with criminals in a foreign tongue

kinds of bilingual programs for children

kinds of language within a single group

kinds of comic-page devices for humor

kinds of testimonials

things done to poke fun at politicians

kinds of touch

kinds of ways to express the same thing

parts of an essay

parts of a book

kinds of faces you put on depending on your audience

kinds of editing

kinds of occupational titles

kinds of city language

kinds of country language

ways of "mis-speaking" (regarding the term that came out of Watergate)

kinds of ways words get started

kinds of language within a single country

Work, Customs, and Ways of People

unpleasant journalistic types

kinds of people I like

kinds of people I dislike

people in television ads

people in television shows

people at the stage theatre

kinds of workers

kinds of bores

friendly festival of fall

familiar faces

the three cultures of the Papagos

doctor, lawyer, merchant, chief, tinker, tailor, etc.

kinds of crowds

kinds of city folk

kinds of editors

old friends, new friends, forever friends

movie audiences

kinds of TV hosts

kinds of workers in television

USSR—its makeup

the greatest _____

psychologist, psychiatrist, psychoanalyst, etc.

small ambitions

kinds of country folk

kinds of companions

kinds of salespersons in different parts of the country

kinds of clowns

celebrity models

singing/courting customs in Latin America

the staff of the White House

drinkers, chewers, walkers, runners, conversationalists, jokers

Classification/Division items may be drawn from these quotations:

"In the language of screen comedians," said James Agee, "four of the main grades of laugh are the titter, the yowl, the belly laugh, and the boffo. The titter is just a titter. A yowl is a runaway titter. Anyone who has ever had the pleasure knows all about the belly laugh. The boffo is the laugh that kills."

"At night all cats are grey," says a proverb.

"Broadly speaking," said Winston Churchill, "human beings may be divided into three classes: those who are toiled to death, those who are worried to death, and those who are bored to death."

"Children in ordinary dress," said Hilaire Belloc, "may always play with sand."

"One religion is as true as another," said Robert Burton.

"To every thing there is a season," says Ecclesiastes.

"The more alternatives, the more difficult the choice," said D'Allainval.

"At twenty years of age," said Benjamin Franklin, "the will reigns; at thirty, the wit; and at forty, the judgment."

"Occupational specialization in some countries is precise by law," said W. D. Powell, "so that the tobacconist sells only tobacco and the repair shop is licensed to repair only second-hand bicycles."

"Everybody has his own theatre, in which he is manager, actor, prompter, playwright, sceneshifter, boxkeeper, doorkeeper, all in one, and audience into the bargain," said Julius and Augustus Hare.

Walter Bagehot said: "Wordsworth, Tennyson, and Browning: or, Pure, Ornate, and Grotesque Art in English Poetry."

Philip James Bailey said: "America, thou half-brother of the world;/With something good and bad of every land."

"There are four classes of Idols which beset men's minds," said Sir Francis Bacon. "To these for distinction's sake I have assigned names—calling the first class, Idols of the Tribe; the second, Idols of the Cave; the third, Idols of the Market-place; the fourth, Idols of the Theatre."

"The night has a thousand eyes," said Francis Bourdillon.

"Life is made up of sobs, sniffles, and smiles, with sniffles predominating," said O. Henry.

"Nations, like men, have their infancy," said Henry St. John, Viscount Bolingbroke.

"Nations touch at their summits," said Walter Bagehot.

CAUSE AND EFFECT

What Cause and Effect Writing Is

Cause and effect are correlative terms and they are immensely useful as a rhetorical combination: if this and this and this happen the more or less natural result will be that (the effect). Or, to turn the technique on its deductive head, *that* happens because of this and this and this. It is easy to see how a piece of writing could be constructed along these lines. In fact, entire philosophical systems have been erected from cause and effect structures, at least from the time Aristotle attempted what may have been the first full explanation of the principle of causality.

How to Write Cause and Effect

Identify the fact, the person, thing or condition, describe how that circumstance brings about the more or less natural result, and you will find yourself in the midst of writing cause and effect. The method is orderly and, it would seem, obvious; but twentieth-century physics has brought the notion of causality into question. Causality is probably still useful for measuring reality on a large scale, in terms of space and time (such and such will lead to majority rule in South Africa), but that kind of measurement is no longer possible on an atomic scale. There is no apparent order in the reality of elementary particles. There—in what would seem to be the material essence of the matter (of *all* matter)—chaos rules. And there is no known way of measuring that chaos beyond a certain point without the measurer's becoming a part of the measurement.

This is not the diversion it may appear. Writers—especially those in a country that sometimes prides itself on the illusion of objectivity—would do well to remember that in its material depths the only reality we know is chaotic. Our relationship with that reality is, therefore, necessarily subjective. The effect is humbling: Suddenly writing is no longer a way of pontificating the answers. It becomes instead a way of exploring reality, of interrogating being. Writing from cause and effect can still be an orderly method of interrogating something, but in the long run we can no longer expect it to explain much of anything.

So what, though, if we cannot undo, or get rid of, chaos? There is more gain than loss even here, in the writing of cause and effect. Writing helps us to see what is and, so far as is humanly possible, to deal with it as it is. When there is a risk involved, a confrontation with chaos, when something personally vital is on the line, then some of the mystery and some of the wonder of writing are restored. Mystery and wonder are what living language is all about, logic and order notwithstanding.

Locating Subjects for Cause and Effect

This chapter is one of the most substantial in the book. Almost anything can be interrogated through cause and effect. The approach to this device can easily bring together process, research and report, argumentation, and expository writing. It can also be put to a more explicitly creative use, however. Consider a mystery story, for example, working its way backwards from the corpse to the first cause, the prime mover of the deed. Or, to turn the order around, consider a story tragic in a classical sense, where the inherent faults (causes) in a character of whatever nobility affect his eventual downfall.

Clearly, cause and effect can be crafted in various ways, but we would do well *especially in this kind of writing* to let go of our opinion that everything is as ordered as it seems to be.

Art, Drama, Music, Graphics, Film, etc.

Why is _____ considered such an accomplished artist?

What is the effect of experience on art?

What is the effect of war on art? On creativity?

What is the effect of the emotions on art? On creativity?

Why are some artists "discovered" only posthumously?

What would cause (or what *did* cause) a great producer, director, or actor to make a bad movie?

Discuss in cause-and-effect terms the moral dilemma of an actor who is asked to take a role of an evil person —say, of a Nazi war criminal.

Discuss in cause-and-effect terms the fact that in the movie world "you have to have talent, you have to work hard, and it is well to have a talent for luck."

Discuss in cause-and-effect terms the belief that we all have a little of the musician, the poet, and the crazy person in us.

Why is pottery a key to understanding past cultures?

Why do the works of a certain important artist affect you?

Assume that there is always an explanation for a like or a dislike, and tell why you like or dislike a certain work of art.

Through cause and effect, relate psychiatry (*not* psycho-drama) to drama.

Where does the inspiration of a song come from? Which comes first, words or music? What things are there all around us that, not taken for granted, could supply us with material for songs?

As an exercise in sensual description, listen to a favorite piece of music and write a description of the effects of the music on *all* your senses. Obviously you will describe the sounds, but also bring your other senses into play: What visual images does the music cause (or create)? What smells, tastes, or textures? What particular details of the music cause these sensations and associations?

Why did John Bampfylde say, "Rugged the breast that beauty cannot tame"?

What cause-and-effect lesson is there in the fact that Pandora opened the box?

Why is the art world usually considered as separate from the "real" world?

Why do we look up to the stars—that is, movie stars and singing stars?

Why do we spend time on art that might be spent more practically?

Why is a certain television show an unexpected success?

Why does something seen over and over still strike some people as funny?

What drains the life out of creativity?

Why would you want, or not want, to judge the work of your classmates or to have them judge your work?

Biology, Botany, Chemistry, etc.

What effects does oxygen or some other chemical element have on plants?

What effects do enzymes have on human physiology?

What causes food to spoil?

What damage does a certain non-human creature cause?

Why are animal instincts not always best for certain animals?

Explain the scientific observation that complex animals survive less well than simple animals do.

What does ecology do for us?

Why do jumping beans jump?

Why did the dinosaurs become extinct? Why have creatures in modern times become extinct?

Business, Office or Bureaucracy

What does industry do (or what can it do) to prevent routine from becoming depressing for its employees?

Show why, according to the Bible, "in all labor there is profit."

Why should one get a job?

Why can, according to Cervantes, "Many littles make one big"?

Why do smallcraft flying accidents occur mostly among business people?

Why are airline prices as they are now?

Why is time considered money? Why is money considered time? What would be the effect of your investing time?

What causes computers to send out money to the wrong persons? Does this explain why computers sometimes do not send out money to the right persons?

Why do workers who gripe so much succeed in their work better than those who do not?

A Hallmark item says: "A little determination is behind each big success." Isn't it more accurate to say just the opposite?—"A lot of determination is behind each little success."

Why has it been said that "losing a job can be the first step towards a new and better job"?

What comes of being in the right place at the right time?

Does wealth desired for its own sake obstruct the increase of virtue, as Woolman believed?

Does avarice spur industry, as David Hume argued?

Is hunger the best cook, as a proverb says?

What would be the effect(s) of your putting off until tomorrow some important task that you have been advised to do today?

What comes from buying wristwatches in cigar stores?

Why does inflation affect the cost of books?

What causes either the end of plenty or the end of a certain shortage?

What are the effects of inflation on people whose incomes are fixed?

Why do real estate prices rise and fall?

What effects did the New Deal have on the wealthy? On the poor?

In cause-and-effect terms, discuss the Biblical statement, "Money answers all things."

Discuss a headline that reads, Gold Fever Still Strikes.

Is turmoil the effect of progress? Is it therefore the price of progress?

Why would the Better Business Bureau caution against buying plants by mail?

Why might Joseph Addison have said that "A good face is a letter of recommendation"?

What is the status of the solar-energy business? What is its status the effect of?

Why is it true that "All is not gold that glitters"?

Why do some businesses fail during hard times?

What causes a decline in the quality of merchandise sold to a mass market?

Why has the reputation of the hotdog declined in recent years?

"A hungry rooster doesn't cackle when it finds a worm," said Joel Chandler Harris. Explain what effects "cackling" in the business world would have.

Children

Why do children run away from children's institutions? From home?

Why do children go *right*?

What effects, if any, does television violence have on children?

Why do children behave as they do towards certain offenses?

Why is it assumed by some that an only child will be spoiled?

Why do siblings quarrel?

Why do the very young distrust or dislike some people over thirty?

What are the effects on children who have been—like Brer Rabbit—"born and bred in a brier-patch"?

What is the effect on the child of one sex who knows that the parent(s) favored another sex?

Why does the exotic appeal to children?

Why is it possible for children to solve social problems they have not learned about by experience?

Why do children need more "quality time" with their parents?

What causes delinquency in children?

Why do children imitate the habits of their parents? Why do children learn?

In the words of a song by Rodgers and Hammerstein, children "have to be carefully taught" to have preju-

dice. Is prejudice something that children learn? Can tolerance be learned?

Does television teach children (as it has been argued) bribery, bad grammar, bad language, bad manners, and bad diet?

Economics

What effects does trucking have on the economy? What effects does the economy have on trucking?

What is behind the increase/decrease of _____ in the economy?

Do income taxes kill the golden goose?

What causes certain jobs to fail during hard times? What causes certain jobs to hold up during both good times and bad?

Is it so that, as Benjamin Franklin said, "Necessity never made a good bargain"?

Why did a certain economic measure fail?

Is it so that "Poverty's catching," as Aphra Behn said?

"Change is not made without inconvenience, even from worse to better," said Richard Hooker. Apply this cause-and-effect argument to economics.

What caused a recent stock increase or decrease?

Do inflated salaries cause inflation?

What is the prediction for the economy five years from now? Why?

What effects do natural conditions such as drought or heavy snow have on the economy?

Why is it true in economics that "Every cost has its own wearing"?

Education

What effects does education have on *you*?

Why can students in these times say after their education, All of that for *nothing*?

Why is it assumed that a university degree assures the graduate of a better life?

What problems might the bored student cause?

Why are there so many special activities in schools?

What effects, if any, does knowledge have on us?

Why might added words make for added knowledge or wisdom?

Why might criticism teach condemnation?

Why might hostility teach belligerence?

Why might fear teach apprehension?

Why might pity teach self-pity?

Why might jealousy teach guilt?

Why might encouragement teach confidence?

Why might tolerance teach patience?

Why might praise teach appreciation?

Why might approval teach self-respect?

Why might acceptance teach love?

Why might recognition teach goals?

Why might fairness teach justice?

Why might honesty teach truth?

Why might security teach faith in self?

Why might friendliness teach friendliness?

Why might eyes and mind work together to educate?

Why might much study, as the Bible says, "dull"?

Why might learning often come from the strangest or least likely experience?

Why, according to the Bible, can the truth make you free?

Why do some think that it pays to be ignorant?

Why are community colleges gaining ground over traditional colleges?

Why, according to Sir Francis Bacon, is knowledge power?

Why are low test scores among students of a certain area obstacles for keeping industry out of the area?

What could cause us to love reading more? to hate it more?

Why has learning "gained most by those books which the printers have lost," as Thomas Fuller said?

What is the consequence of the fact that, as Heracleitus said, "All is flux, nothing is fixed"?

Does a learning problem necessarily cause a learning disability?

What effects do private schools have on public education?

Why did Blake think that "The road of excess leads to the palace of wisdom"?

Why is it considered that the one who knows much knowledge knows much sorrow?

What causes graduation depression?

What causes the current deep despair among professors?

What effect(s) does Socrates have on modern students?

What effect(s) does Aristotle have on modern students?

Why do we place education over house and land?

What are the effects of learning in a closet rather than in the world?

Why is it said that everything has been said already?

Why is it said that we are thousands of years too late in our education?

Why can we not learn from books about human nature?

Discuss in terms of cause and effect the statement by Disraeli, "Experience is the child of Thought, and Thought is the child of Action."

Discuss in terms of cause and effect the statement by Goethe, "Treat people as if they were what they ought to be and you help them to become what they are capable of being."

Discuss in terms of cause and effect the statement by Robert Frost, "I go to school to youth to learn the future."

Discuss: You have to carry knowledge with you if you want to bring knowledge home.

What causes us to dislike learning facts? Is it in part because we would (perhaps unknowingly) prefer to create them instead?

Why is it necessary to educate for democracy?

Mechanical facility is the effect of what kind of intelligence?

What comes of learning without preconceptions?

Why can learning be an effect of dialogue or conversation?

What will be, or what would be, the effects of a nation-wide "scientific illiteracy"?

What would be the effect of learning a little bit of adversity at a time?

What would be the teaching effects if _____ (some public figure) were a teacher?

Knowledge helps us "escape the hell of subjectivity," said Samuel Johnson. Why should that be so?

"I have not thoughts enough to think," said John Ford. Discuss this statement in terms of cause and effect.

What causes experience, and what does experience cause?

What was an early explanation of why learning works as it does?

"Age teaches," says a Spanish proverb. What does age teach?

"A few words only are necessary for the good learner," says a Spanish proverb. Why?

"No one is deafer than the one who does not choose to hear," says a Spanish proverb. Discuss this statement in terms of cause and effect.

"Wisdom denotes the pursuing of the best ends by the best means," said Francis Hutcheson. Discuss this statement in terms of cause and effect.

Discuss whether in education "better late than never" applies.

In what way will *society* be affected by *your* education?

What effects do the college-bred have on social values?

Discuss in terms of cause and effect: "The first wrote, Wine is strongest. The second wrote, The King is strongest. The third wrote, Women are strongest: but above all things Truth beareth away the victory." —Bible.

Discuss in terms of cause and effect: "All the choir of heaven and furniture of earth—in a word, all those bodies which compose the mighty frame of the world—have not any subsistence without a mind."—Bishop Berkeley.

Ethics and Philosophy

Discuss this quotation from William Blake: "Everything that lives,/Lives not alone, nor for itself."

Discuss this quotation from Benjamin Franklin: "There never was a good war, or a bad peace."

Discuss this quotation from Sir Robert Aytoun: "You are not what you were before: what reason is there that I should be the same?"

"Life demands to be lived," said H.L. Mencken. Is this the answer to the question, Why do we remain active?

Is there ever "a victim of circumstance"?

Discuss this quotation from the ancient philosopher, Boethius: "In adverse fortune the worst sting of misery is to have been happy."

Discuss from either side of the ambiguity/ambivalence the statement that nothing comes from nothing.

Discuss whether or not ideas always have consequences.

Discuss whether it is possible for good to exist without evil or for evil to exist without good.

What is the effect of having someone else's thoughts in your mind?

Why can adversity be described as "bread"?

Why do weak protests sometimes equal no protests?

Discuss whether or not it is true that, according to Byron, the weak alone repent.

Explain in terms of cause and effect what Shakespeare meant by the comment that conscience makes cowards of us all.

Discuss the Spanish proverb that says that it is better to lose a moment of life than to lose life in a moment.

Why do some people need keys to open doors that are already open?

Was Browning right in saying, "Truth never hurts the teller"?

Does oppression make the wise person mad, as Robert Browning said?

Is humanity the sole mistake of Nature, as Sir William Gilbert said?

Does virtue breed happiness, as Benjamin Franklin claimed?

Discuss mind over matter/matter over mind in terms of cause and effect.

Show whether it is true in life that when one door closes, others open.

Is it human nature to enjoy the struggle more than the achievement?

Discuss whether it is true that, as Thomas Hardy said, life offers, only to deny.

Is it better to lose with friends than to win with enemies?

Discuss the statement by Dr. George Polya, a mathematician, that "Everything is just a guess, concerning your job, your home, your family, even the laws of physics."

An idea from Edward Fitzgerald's translation of *Omar Khayyam* is that "The flower that once has blown for ever dies." Discuss in terms of cause and effect.

Is it better, as a Spanish proverb says, to be loved than not hated?

Is it so, as a Spanish proverb says, that one who walks from flower to flower will finally choose the worst?

Discuss Thomas Henry Huxley's position that "It is the customary fate of new truths to begin as heresies and to end as superstitions."

Discuss in terms of cause and effect the statement by John Fletcher: "Death hath so many doors to let out life."

What are the effects of the condition that, according to the Spanish proverb, the first one to get wet has more time to get dry?

Why do people seek success? Why do people fear success?

Why is time an "effect" of life? Discuss Benjamin Franklin's comment: "If you love life, do not squander time, of which life is made."

Discuss this statement by Beaumarchais: "I make myself laugh at everything, for fear of having to weep."

Discuss this statement by Jean De La Fontaine: "What does it profit to know the world but not oneself?"

Why does it take life to love life, as Edgar Lee Masters declares in one of his poems?

Is life or death-after-life the effect of living? Why?

What is necessary in this world to enjoy the next?

Why, according to Goethe, does a useless life die early?

What is the effect of the pursuit of perfection?

What is the effect of pursuing "sweetness and light," as Matthew Arnold used the term?

What effect does freedom have on human relationships?

Discuss in cause-and-effect terms the observation by Emerson that "The reward of a thing well done, is to have done it."

Why would you be satisfied, or not be satisfied, with enough if others did not have more?

Trace the cause-and-effect reasoning or the events behind your believing as you do on a particular.

Discuss this statement by Fontenelle: "If I enclosed truths with my hands, I would be wary not to open them."

Discuss this statement by Sir Thomas Browne: "The long habit of living indisposes us for dying."

Discuss this statement by Franklin: "The one who lives on hope dies fasting."

What led Huckleberry Finn to say, "All right, then, I'll go to hell. . . ."?

Why does our inability to conceive of the size of the universe lead us back to thinking about ourselves?

Do you control circumstance, or are you controlled *by* it?

Discuss in cause-and-effect terms the Spanish proverb, "It is good to be important, but it is more important to be good."

Is Disraeli's opinion correct that "Adventures are to the adventurers"?

Are Julius and Augustus Hare correct in saying that "Half the failures in life arise from pulling in one's horse as it is leaping"?

Have moral standards been affected by birth control?

Is there philosophical comfort in this opinion (modernized from Stephen Hawes)?—"For though the day is ever so long,/At last the bells ring to evensong."

"They love their land because it is their own," said Fitz-Greene Halleck. What effects does belonging to something have on us?

If you help yourself, will heaven help you, as Jean De La Fontaine declared?

Discuss the Spanish proverb, "Man proposes, God disposes, and the devil discomposes."

Discuss the declaration by Sir Francis Bacon, "Prosperity doth best discover vice, but adversity doth best discover virtue."

A newspaper headline reads: Decline, Indifference Busts Hall of Fame. Why has the Hall of Fame experienced a decline?

What does it mean, in cause-and-effect terms, to "keep your mind level" when "life's path is steep"? (This idea is paraphrased from Horace.)

What is the first impulse that makes people believe in, or want to believe in, immortality?

Why does tradition exercise such a powerful hold on us?

What associations do most people make about the great questions in life—about love, death, money, and life?

Why can intended good at times be harmful?

Do we try too hard to make it in the world and thus allow too much good to pass us by?

Why does the question "What if?" arouse such interest?

Government, Politics

Why, in voting, is a political incumbent usually favored to win?

"What is past my help is past my care," said John Fletcher. Does this view explain why people take the attitude they take towards politics?

Why do friends (and relatives) in politics sometimes cause more trouble than enemies?

Will changing a bureaucracy cause more bureaucracy?

Discuss "The Will of the People, and the Won't."

What ails (now, or at any time) the American spirit?

Why should the public have baloney detectors?

Why is it said of politicians that "the good are half-bad, and the bad are half-good"?

Why is it so that, as Richard Hooker said, "One who goes about to persuade people that they are not as well-governed as they ought to be will always have listeners"?

What effect does bureaucracy have on idealism?

What effect does idealism have on bureaucracy?

Why might it be said that the government hires stalling experts?

In politics why is it so that (as James Anthony Froude said) "Experience teaches slowly, and at the cost of mistakes"?

In cause-and-effect terms, answer Jack Anderson's question, "What is happening to the American dream?"

Why does common interest not always determine what happens in a democracy?

Why do the computers, rather than the people, sometimes pick the political winner?

Why should poll centers be required to use the Chippewa language when no one can write in it?

Discuss Jeremy Bentham's statement, "The greatest happiness of the greatest number is the foundation of morals and legislation."

Tell what caused certain U.S. Congress members or Senators to leave office willingly rather than pursue other terms.

Discuss what makes stories of political chicanery so interesting.

What effects will government have on education in the near future?

What would be the possible consequences of refusing to reveal (to a judge, say, under a mandate of you) a secret vote?

Why has the unpopularity of Nixon been blamed on his California heritage?

Apply to politics the cause-and-effect Spanish proverb, "The one who walks with wolves will learn to howl."

What did regional backgrounds of certain presidents do to affect their presidential tenures?

Why cannot it be argued that politicians who receive only 51 percent of the vote should have to keep only 51 percent of their promises?

Why does the government not provide until it gets around to providing?

What effects does being president have on the president? What does the presidency do to or for the moral stature of the person holding the office?

What has caused aristocracies to fail?

What brought about the downfall of _____?

Is it true in politics at any level that, as the Bible says, "A soft answer turns away wrath"?

Why is government affected by semantics?

Why does reason teach/not teach in government and politics?

What happens to military personnel who challenge the military?

What happens to government personnel who challenge the government?

Discuss in terms of government and politics the Biblical quotation, "One thousand shall flee at the rebuke of one."

Why did a certain government or country come into being?

Why do figures in government and politics come and go?

Health

What are causes of acne?

Why is acne more than skin deep?

Why does coffee affect you as it does?

What are the effects of rest and time off as remedies for health?

What are the effects of a smoker's stopping smoking?

Why do miscarriages happen?

What causes kitchen accidents? bathroom accidents?

What are the causes and effects of botulism?

What causes hiccups, snoring, the common cold, asthma, insomnia?

What is a cure for each of the conditions noted just above? What unusual cure(s) do you know of?

Why should one try to prevent colds?

Why is sound body related to sound mind?

What cause-and-effect relationship is there between exercise and the nerves?

Why do the Finns have a high rate of heart problems?

Why do most heart attacks occur when they do?

Why is "happiness the sister of health"?

Why do eating habits affect health?

What are some of the different causes of heart disease?

Discuss these quotations from Sir Francis Bacon: "Cure the disease and kill the patient." "The remedy is worse than the disease."

Why was the frontal lobotomy outlawed?

What can be the bad effects of too much tickling?

Why does litter affect the health?

Why does one have to know the cause of something before suggesting its remedy?

History

Why are there so few great men and women?

Why has there been less exodus to Latin America in recent years?

Why will Turkey be less visited than before?

Why will Iran be less visited than before?

Why do certain well-known proverbs not apply in today's world?

What made the 1960s a decade of violence?

Discuss Agathon's quotation, "Even God cannot change the past."

What cause-and-effect connection was there between slavery and "Manifest Destiny"?

In history, has force been a remedy?

Discuss Thomas Jefferson's quotation, "The tree of liberty must be refreshed from time to time with the blood of patriots and tyrants. It is its natural manure."

Why was a certain city or a certain university founded?

Why was there such a delay in ending the Korean War?

What positive effects in human rights would we see today if slavery had really ended with the Civil War?

Explain why Thomas Jefferson is so maligned.

Explain why Thomas Jefferson is so admired.

Explain why Franklin Delano Roosevelt is so maligned.

Explain why Franklin Delano Roosevelt is so admired.

What, specifically, do we gain from learning about history?

How have changes wrought by humanity altered the face of the earth and changed the lives of human beings?

Explain why a certain great historical event came about.

Associate by cause and effect terrorism and censorship.

Point up some present influence from a past idea.

Discuss William Hazlitt's quotation, "The temple of fame stands upon the grave: the flame that burns upon its altars is kindled from the ashes of the great."

Discuss Edmund Burke's quotation, "You can never plan the future by the past."

Show what caused someone to be accidentally thrust into greatness.

What will be the causes of World War III?

What will be the effects of World War III?

What were the causes and effects of the Spanish American War?

What were the causes and effects of the Spanish Civil War?

Why are most predictions ominous?

What results in history are always uncertain of prediction?

Why might one think of history—as Daisy Ashford referred to it—as "piffle before the wind"?

What drove the explorers to explore?

Discuss Thomas Paine's quotation, "Every quiet method for peace hath been ineffectual."

What cause-effect tests might be used to determine whether or not a current event will be historically significant?

What cause-effect judgment can we make to place responsibility on past generations for ethical behavior?

Why is it thought that earlier generations were less enlightened morally than we are?

Why has recent history given vindication for someone or something wronged in the past?

What is behind a prediction by one of the modern prophets?

Why should we view history with the phrase "truth or consequences" in mind?

A certain newspaper printed good news one day and retracted it the next. What does this action say about the effect of news in the modern world?

Why does historical "chance" change so often?

Is it true that, as the Spanish proverb says, nothing bad lasts one hundred years?

What—considering recent history—are the future effects of tradition?

Why do we worry so much about other countries?

In recent history, where have we come from and where are we going?

Discuss Thomas Henry Huxley's quotation, "Logical consequences are the scarecrows of fools and the beacons of [the] wise."

Discuss in cause-and-effect terms these words by Robert Frost (delivered at President Kennedy's inaugural): "The land was ours before we were the land's."

Discuss with reference to history the quotation by William Norman Ewer, "I gave my life for freedom— This I know:/For those who bade me fight had told me so."

What happened, as far as archeology and history show, to Sodom and Gomorrah?

What has become of the great lights among Americans during the last ten or fifteen years? What caused them to continue rising in esteem, or to fall?

Discuss the Giordano Bruno quotation, "If it is not true, it is a happy invention."

What have been the effects, historically, of "gentle persuasion"?

What has reason taught/not taught to history?

Discuss in historical cause-and-effect terms Chaucer's quotation, "It is not good a sleeping hound to wake."

Is custom, as David Hume said, the "great guide of human life"?

Discuss historically these words by Marshal Foch:
   "My center is giving way.
   My right is running away:
   My situation is excellent:
   I shall attack!"

Discuss, with reference to history, these lines by Bret Harte:
   "If, of all words of tongue and pen,
   The saddest are, 'It might have been,'
   More sad are these we daily see:
   'It is, but hadn't ought to be!' "

Interpret in cause-and-effect terms the quotation by Carlyle, "Happy the people whose annals are blank in history-books!"

Discuss the historian Edward Gibbon's saying, "Whatsoever might be the future date of my History, the life of the historian must be short and precarious."

Why should Aristotle have considered poetry as "something more philosophic and of graver import than history"?

Why might someone be made, in Thomas Hood's words, "Mad from life's history"?

Discuss in terms of cause and effect Carlyle's quotation, "What is all knowledge too but recorded experience, and a product of history; of which, therefore, reasoning and belief, no less than action and passion, are essential materials?"

Discuss why Carlyle considered "History is the essence of innumerable biographies."

Discuss Disraeli's quotation, "Assassination has never changed the history of the world."

Language

Why did language begin?

Why do new times bring new language(s)?

Does language make its user, or does the user of it make language?

What makes a "dead language"?

What social factors influence language change?

Why are parts of speech and spelling related?

Why are vocabulary and spelling related?

Discuss "Translation and Diplomacy" and "Interpretation and Diplomacy."

Explain why English was not replaced by French after the Norman Conquest of England in 1066.

Using cause and effect, trace the general path of the English language from its beginnings to the present.

What is the cause-and-effect path by which thought becomes language?

Why does legal language read as it does?

Why does our body speak for us?

Why do people who are fluent in a foreign language and its dialects still have severe difficulties communicating with the people who use that language and its dialects?

To what extent and why does "inflammatory language" inflame?

What causes semantic problems?

What causes semantic changes?

Aphra Behn said, "Money speaks sense in a language all nations understand." Why can language be considered money and money be considered language?

Examine the cause-and-effect relationship in any non-word language (such as "the language of the heart").

Why is one language or another gaining supremacy in the world market?

Why is one language or another gaining supremacy in world politics?

Law, Crime

Why is crime in one area greater, or less great, than in another?

What would happen if everyone were a lawmaker?

What would happen if there were no laws, restrictions, or police?

What is the effect of law by vigilantes?

Discuss the result of a certain recent investigation.

What accounts for the belief that "a police officer is never around when needed"?

Are criminals born, or made?

Are law abiders born, or made?

Are some laws such that *anyone* can be thrown into jail?

Why did crime break out in the streets during a blackout of power in a major city?

What is gained, if anything, by punishing criminals or lesser offenders of the law?

What is the *usual* cause behind a murder?

What effects do criminal parents have on their families?

Why do old statutes remain on the books?

What causes police brutality (or what allows it to happen) where it occurs?

Discuss the probable result of following the Biblical quotation, "Love is the fulfilling of the law."

Discuss the probable result of following the quotation by Edmund Burke, "Liberty must be limited in order to be possessed."

Why are all of us affected by major crimes?

What causes child abuse?

What are the effects of the law on child abusers?

Why are there inequities in the law in the way the poor and the rich are treated?

Explain why a certain mystery from some decades back remains unsolved.

Literature, Writing

Why should it be true that, as Leon Uris the writer has said, "Fortunately, English and writing have little to do with each other"?

Show why fairy tales prove or disprove themselves in our daily lives.

Why is the typewriter said to take over the writer's control?

Why might an active writer not read anything but her/his own work?

Write an essay entitled "Let Me Be Your Maker," in which you attempt to show how literature can manipulate others, for good or bad.

What "causes" literature?

What are the effects of literature?

What benefits result from literature? Are people changed for the better by moral literature, that is, literature which demonstrates what ethical behavior ought to be?

What effect(s) can one word have?

Why does Las Vegas give better odds than the odds against publishing a first novel?

What are the effects of a report that is easy to understand?

What are the effects of a report that is hard to understand?

Why do many people not like literature?

Why does literature that has an underhanded purpose not read simply?

Why are Homer, Dante, Milton, and Shakespeare difficult to read?

Explain in cause-and-effect terms the quotation by Sir Arthur Helps, "Reading is sometimes an ingenious device for avoiding thought."

Discuss Milton's statement that one who destroys a good book "kills reason itself."

Why did Bacon say that writing makes one "exact"?

Media

Why do networks play down certain world news?

What are the effects of advertising?

Why do advertisements often have such little connection with reality?

Why might someone reasonably say after watching a bad television show, "I think I'll learn to read?"

What are the effects of the "hidden persuaders" in the media?

Why do newspapers lose readers?

Why are people gullible about the news?

Why does cigarette advertising make smokers out of non-smokers?

What impact has television had on education?

What impact has television had on thought?

Why is television the opiate of the masses?

What accounts for the decline in readership of a certain magazine?

Why do magazines and newspapers collapse? What has caused the collapse of a particular magazine or newspaper that was very famous?

Why is advertising capable of manipulating people?

Why are certain facts released only gradually by the media?

Why is _____ the most popular magazine in the world?

Why is _____ the most popular television program in the country?

What is the influence of the media in national politics?

Why does newspaper readership increase even in certain areas where there are many television watchers?

Discuss the effects of the development of printing.

Discuss in cause-and-effect terms the professional laughers (who are hired to inspire laughter in the audience) who exist in the television world.

What is the effect of selling reputations through the media?

Why are we controlled by the movie industry and the television industry?

Why do soap operas appeal to so many?

What are the effects of the "news game" that television plays?

Discuss the quotation by the television commentator Sander Vanocur, "How do you balance the necessity to be entertaining but at the same time informative about television?"

Discuss the quotation by Arnold Bennett, "Journalists say a thing that they know isn't true, in the hope that if they keep on saying it long enough it _will_ be true."

Why does "public service" advertising help big business?

What did prophets of early television see that caused many of their predictions about television to come true?

Physical Science

What causes "acid rain"?

What are the causes of a certain weather condition?

What are the effects of a certain weather condition?

What are the causes and effects of "star death"?

What causes tornados?

What causes steaming of glass?

What positive effects can come from the study of astronomy?

What causes smog? What can prevent smog?

What are the positive effects of having been to the moon?

What causes "leaking electricity"?

Why can it be argued (not seriously, of course) that the groundhog makes the weather?

Is there any effect in physical science for which there is no cause? Does everything in the world having to do with physical science have a cause?

Discuss Robert Ingersoll's quotation, "In nature there are neither rewards nor punishments—there are consequences."

Why is it, as Sherlock Holmes says, "a capital mistake to theorize before one has data"?

What scientific evidence, if any, exists to indicate the time and cause of the end of the world?

What effect has Rachel Carson's *Silent Spring* had on the world?

What was the cause behind a certain major power failure?

Discuss the cartoon question, "Was the one who discovered fire the first to pollute the atmosphere?"

Discuss the Thomas Henry Huxley quotation, "The great tragedy of Science—the slaying of a beautiful hypothesis by an ugly fact."

Discuss the quotation by Dr. George Polya, a mathematician, "What is the scientific method except Guess and Test?"

Drawing from the range of both superstition and fact, discuss some element of scientific revolution.

Psychology

Why are stories of near-death experiences fascinating to most of us?

What motivates courage?

What motivates fear?

Why does losing breed losing?

Why does winning breed winning?

Why do those who have been burned emotionally react as they do?

Why is it, as Jean De La Fontaine says, "a double pleasure . . . to deceive the deceiver"?

What caused _____ to come emotionally into its/her/his/their own?

Why does Mexico have so many road and train accidents?

Why do some psychiatrists say there is no such thing as an accident?

Why can a single person by sway of personality influence many others?

What psychological effect is there in standing over someone?

What are the effects of having a psychological edge on someone?

Discuss in cause-effect terms the friction between two famous people.

Why do we acquire habits? What causes habit to rule our lives?

Why does persuasion work as it does?

Why does the unexpected happen?

Why does the simple often become difficult?

What good results can we have by applying animal behavior to human behavior?

Why do dogs have a sense of whom to trust?

Why do animals (since they are without our mental capacity) have psychological problems?

Why did a certain experiment with animals lead to a better understanding of them?

Why does "But . . ." sometimes cancel out the words before it in the minds of those who hear it?

What is the reason behind a bully's behavior?

Is there a psychological explanation for the fact that many of the mechanical things you try are out of order?

Discuss Hilaire Belloc's saying, "A lost thing could I never find,/Nor a broken thing mend."

Why are "Some people . . . so fond of ill-luck that they run half-way to meet it," as Douglas Jerrold said?

Which makes the individual: heredity, or environment?

Why do wives/husbands/children run away?

What explains why some people choose one part of the room to sit in and other people choose another?

Why do smiles, winks, or sympathetic grunts affect us as they do?

Why do some people who have nothing to say talk anyhow?

What are the effects of a good/a bad sense of humor?

Explain what causes employers to react as they do to prospective employees who have a history of illness or who have been in prison.

What causes one phobia or another? What are its effects?

What causes one mania or another? What are its effects?

What causes an obsession? What are its effects?

Explain what psychological factors were responsible for a good/a bad turnout for a recent event—an election, for example, or a major athletic event.

Why do we forget where we put things?

Why do we forget what we did?

Why do we deceive ourselves in thinking that time spent on an effort is all we need to accomplish it?

What accounted for the fact that a certain day of yours went wrong/right?

Why do you feel/not feel at home at _____?

Why does love stoop in order to rise, as Robert Browning has said?

Why does love cease to be a pleasure, as Aphra Behn says, "when it ceases to be a secret"?

Why does the world have little to offer "where two fond hearts in equal love are joined," as Anna Barbould said?

Discuss the opinion of Samuel Butler that " 'Tis better to have loved and lost, than never to have lost at all."

Discuss in psychological cause-effect terms the quotation from Thomas Becon, "When the wine is in, the wit is out."

Why are happy surprises good for us?

Why do we need praise to do well?

Why do insignificant memories sometimes take precedence over important ones?

Why does laughter help mental health?

Why do we lie about our ages?

What, psychologically, is behind our drive to "save time"?

Why do you and _____ not get along as well as you once did?

Why is self-torture related to self-pity?

Discuss the causes for, and effects of, psychological crutches and psychological retreats.

Why is it accurate, or why is it not accurate, to say "What I'm to be I am now becoming"?

Why can imagination or dreaming make us happy?

What is the cause-effect path in temptation?

Why might there be such a thing as reasonable paranoia?

What makes some people jinxes?

What are the causes and effects of frustration?

Why did B. F. Skinner's "baby box" not revolutionize child-rearing?

Why are some people hynotizable and others are not?

What are the causes and effects of deep despair?

Discuss in psychological cause-effect terms the quotation from Thomas Brown (quoting in translation some lines from Martial): "I do not love you, Dr. Fell,/But why I cannot tell,/But this I know full well,/I do not love you, Dr. Fell."

Why is there a relationship between the individual world and the collective world?

What causes accident proneness?

Why does staying bitter cause more pain?

Why is handwriting analysis valid?

What are the roots of, and causes of, embarrassment?

What psychological phenomenon accounts for charisma?

Why is one kind of death more terrifying than another?

Does television contribute to, or detract from, the thinking process?

What explains the way we write, especially the way we sign our names?

Discuss Froude's statement, "Fear is the parent of cruelty."

Discuss Matthew Arnold's statement, "We forget because we must and not because we will."

Why does crying help us emotionally?

Draw a cause-effect relationship between electricity and the brain.

Why do psychiatrists believe as they do about the relationship between bodily changes and emotions?

Why do those we love have, as John Fletcher said, the "most power to hurt us"?

Write a cause-effect essay on those who are *like* what they *do*: computer technicians who are like computers, for example.

Why can moral strength sometimes come out of psychological weakness?

Why do comedians (not necessarily intentionally) dull our minds to seek out answers ourselves to public issues?

Why do teenagers like noisy dances? (The writer Ray Kytle has said, "They like them because they relieve them of the necessity of having anything to say to their partners.")

What are the causes and effects of anger?

Is cursing a sign of laziness, intelligence, vitality, or what?

Discuss the phenomenon of "behavior control."

Why do certain kinds of sounds or words convey certain feelings?

Why and how does an idea originate?

Discuss the proverb: "Tell me who your friends are and I will tell you who you are."

Is insomnia caused by the fear of falling asleep?

Discuss the statement by John Ford, "Melancholy can turn men into monsters."

Apply this statement by Jean De La Fontaine to psychology: "I bend but do not break."

Discuss this cartoon caption: "I finally got rid of my inferiority complex, but it loosened my grip on reality."

What effects do feelings have on the facial expression?

What effects have advances in medicine had on our fear of (or lack of fear of) death?

What are the roots (or the branches) of our human condition? In other words, what causes us to be as we are?

Why do the eyes speak our emotions or thoughts?

Can sleep be a psychological as well as a physiological remedy?

What are the effects of pain on the mind?

Discuss these lines from William Blake:
"I was angry with my friend
I told my wrath, my wrath did end.

I was angry with my foe:
I told it not, my wrath did grow."

Religion

Why are religions born?

Is morality an effect of religion?

Why do athletes—from opposing teams—pray for victory?

Why is sport considered religious?

Why are there so many major similarities among major religions of the world?

What effect has religion had on a certain period of history?

Can good in the religious sense exercise influence on evil?

Can evil exercise influence on good in the religious sense?

What causes a religious believer to see the light? to be reborn?

Why do religious orders provide less escape from the world than before?

What causes anyone to know what the will of God is?

Do the religious convictions of persons determine how much help they are willing to give those in need?

Discuss: "Saints cannot do what God does not want to do."

Discuss this quotation from William Blake, "Love seeks not itself to please."

Why does money have so much to do with religion as it is on television?

Social Science (Sociology, Social Theory, etc.)

Why is it possible to argue with the computer about what you are going to do? about what will happen to you? about what will be done to you?

Discuss the ironic observation about human nature in this quotation from Jane Austen, "It is a truth universally acknowledged, that a single man in possession of a good fortune, must be in want of a wife."

Explain why a certain poll failed.

Why have some people turned against those who were killed at Kent State?

A picture of an innocent bystander at Kent State caused her abuse all over the world. Why do the innocent suffer verbal and physical abuse?

Why do we vote as we do?

What causes giddiness? Why are laughter and yawning contagious?

Why did boy and girl acquaintances of yours break up?

What makes a settlement begin in a place where there is "nothing"?

What causes a strain on mass human relations?

What is ahead in the next few years in marriage-divorce statistics? Why?

Show how *Roots* and *Holocaust* used the small picture (the family) to help the audience grasp the large picture (society, a people, a human condition) more fully.

What effect did *Holocaust* have on audiences in Germany? Why?

What effect did *Roots* have on whites?

Why did Jewish people react as they did to *Holocaust*?

Why did blacks react as they did to *Roots*?

Discuss T. S. Eliot's statement, "I think that the passion for social righteousness will prove in the end not enough in itself."

Do natural surroundings of a people determine what a people will be? Think of Hitler, born in a beautiful setting; think of the poet Ruben Dario, born in an ugly setting.

What will people do, or not do, to gain fame, money, or public office?

Tell what would happen in your life if you lived without pets.

Why do New Englanders have the highest suicide rate in the United States?

Does custom reconcile us to everything, as Edmund Burke declared?

Why do the works of certain authors come into, then fall out of, public favor?

Why are people fascinated with fire-eaters and other daredevils?

Why is convention a state of mind of society?

What effects does convention have on society?

Why do we lie? Why do we make excuses?

What causes death in the ghettos?

Why are beauty pageants popular?

Why are there inequities in public opinion in the way the poor and the rich are considered?

What explains the compulsion we have to be with others? Why is the human being basically not a lone animal?

What are the first concerns and questions among family members united after an exceptionally long separation? Why?

What does its graffiti tell us about a nation or about its individuals?

What social phenomenon is revealed when there is a newly vacant seat on a crowded bus?

Why does the definition of "society" vary from one person to the next?

What common values exist in society, and why?

Is there anything in the regulations of _____ that keeps us from being individuals in society?

What causes us to realize when we are most alone?

Is development of public land always in the best interests of society?

What questions does a poor person have who falls in love with a rich person? Why?

What questions does a rich person have who falls in love with a poor person? Why?

Discuss this quotation from Henry Fielding: "Some folks rail against other folks, because other folks have what some folks would be glad of."

Sports and Physical Activities

Discuss Bill Russell's argument that winning and losing depend more on "chemistry" than on skill or good players.

Why do people jog, or run?

Why do people jog or run less than they did before?

What does jogging *not* do for the jogger?

Why do people who place last in the marathon have any consolation?

Why do people think there is a relationship between athletic ability and name?

Why should a certain baseball player have felt obligated to give up part of his salary while he was in a slump?

What causes hypocrisy in sports?

Define sportsmanship in terms of cause and effect in athletics.

Why don't athletes know their own statistics? Why shouldn't they know, for example, when they are about to break records?

What do athletes think about while they are participating in their sports? Why?

Can nutrition and training make an athlete?

What is behind most sports deaths?

Why is winning so important to most athletes?

Why does one select one sport rather than another?

Why might an athlete prefer to set records rather than help the team win?

What really constitutes or brings about "individual effort" in sports?

What accounted for the fact that a certain sports upset took place?

Are athletes controlled more by themselves, or by circumstances?

What appeals does skiing have for the part-time skier?

What, besides age, causes decline in an athlete?

Can one by intense exercise make up for years of leisure and physical non-activity?

EXPOSITION

What Exposition Is

Exposition is the setting forth of purpose or meaning—not, in a strict sense at least, to criticize, argue, or develop a subject, but to open it up, lay its bones bare. A more literal image of the art might be described as moving the subject out of position, coaxing, jolting, or driving it into a fresh new perspective, so that it will stand more clearly forth and *expose* itself for what it is.

How to Write Exposition

Clarity is essential in exposition. Limit your subject. Keep it tight, unified, concrete. Do all that yet let the subject breathe and you will have turned the trick of exposition. Perhaps that can best be done by allowing the subject to explain itself, expose itself from within, from that depth where the bones are barest. Impose an explanation of your own and there is every chance you will violate that stricter sense of the form. Therefore, this form would probably be better used to explain a subject you know well, rather than to explore something you are only just discovering. In any case, effective exposition is good writing discipline, useful in nearly any other kind of writing and fundamental to most.

Locating Subjects for Exposition

We have held to the stricter sense of exposition here partly because broader senses are more explicitly engaged in other sections of this book. Exposition shares a common root with the word "expound," which also describes a way of presenting a subject. But expounding on a subject will more likely lead beyond bare explanation into interpretation, argumentation, or other critical techniques best considered in their own right. Of course, almost any subject listed in those other chapters is open to an expository treatment in the stricter sense we are struggling to maintain here as well. (It might be helpful to recall that in certain musical forms the "exposition" refers to the first part in which the thematic material is straightforwardly presented. Later in the movement other techniques are used to shape, develop, and adorn that same material.)

An expository essay on *exposition* itself might toughen its *definition* by *contrasting* it with *narration*. It would take a cracking good student essayist to explain a story without explaining it away.

Professions, Occupations

What jobs hold up best during both good times and bad times?

For what is Buckminster Fuller known?

How has prophecy become a profession?

Who ought to be included in a bureau of experts?

Is welding an important profession?

What new field creates many new professions?

Why are civil servants being paid *not* to come to work?

Will changing professions at age fifty be common by the year 2000?

Commerce, Finance, Economy, Economics

What were some common ways of making a common living during the Depression?

How would you treat a customer who came into your store?

How would you behave with a salesperson?

Discuss the growth of conglomerates.

Discuss how debts are paid.

Does the average person have the ability to make a lot of money?

What are some major Medicaid rip-offs?

What are border-town banks like in Latin America?

What is it like for someone to come into a fortune?

What will stores of the future be like?

Are car pools as financially successful as thought?

Discuss Harry S. Truman's fight against hoarding.

What is an occupation from which one can make "big bucks" for long hours?

Discuss big spending.

Discuss money devaluation.

How can one translate the fine print to get rid of rip-offs in bank contracts?

Discuss the battle for control of a certain company.

What are (or what ought to be) oil/gas production incentives?

What are (or what ought to be) tax breaks for individuals? for companies?

What are some calculated billing snares for credit-card holders?

How are the rich stolen from?

Discuss blatant abuses of government-supported student loans.

To what extent does the customer protest affect the price of goods?

Discuss the abuse of expense accounts. Discuss the "martini lunch."

Discuss the death tax that exists in other countries.

What is a venture in which the very young have become financially successful?

What is a new form of business?

What "extras" are offered by the telephone company but not generally known to the public?

_____ are not getting any cheaper/are not getting any easier to come by.

How accurately does Hollywood portray the financial world as it really is?

Why has social security lost its status?

Discuss allowance(s) for dependent children.

Discuss owning a farm.

Why does the computer send money a person has not earned?

How are our tax dollars used?

Discuss television networks and money.

What is a new con game?

What is one of the best-paying fields?

How would the world be different if its material stores were equally divided?

Write of an unusual entrepreneurial venture.

Are you, in these times, "what you own" or "what you owe"?

Write an extended example of how money makes money, or how money buys time.

What state has the best unemployment benefits?

Discuss insurance abuses, from both sides: the consumers and the businesses.

Discuss the growing divorce "business."

How independent is a salesperson?

What are your chances for audit? What happens in an audit?

What is a new form of identifying check-cashers?

What employment prospects are there in the field of ecology?

Will you be a victim of fraud before this week is over?

What are some treasures underfoot?

What are examples of "unreal estate"?

How can one drive a hard bargain?

Discuss taxpayer revolts.

What caused an isolated (that is, not a national) labor-management dispute?

Sports, Entertainment

Is there a way in sports in which both opponents can lose?

How accurately does Hollywood portray the sports world?

Discuss the phenomenon of a new craze or fad.

Discuss a certain sports scandal.

Discuss athletes and religion.

Why do more and more fans stay home and watch sports on television?

Is it true that "there's no business like show business"?

Discuss sports (radio, television) announcers.

Discuss free agents in sports.

Discuss a certain child superstar, such as Tracy Austin or Steve Cauthen.

Discuss time as it applies to the athlete.

Can star athletes as a rule coach well?

What do families do on weekends?

Do sports spectators like violence?

Education

Discuss the battle for control of a certain school or school system.

Be an expert in something and, using the special language associated with it, explain it to someone who is unacquainted with it.

Give to a lay person some understanding of a difficult subject, such as a scientific law.

Discuss logic in education.

Can writing be taught?

Discuss Emerson's quotation, "Never read a book that is not a year old."

Discuss Samuel Butler's quotation, "Learning, that cobweb of the brain,/Profane, erroneous, and vain."

Discuss Joseph Hall's quotation, "Perfection is the child of Time."

What has newly developed to give the blind sight?

How can the mature retarded take care of themselves?

What difficulties do public schools in Washington, D.C. have?

Is it relevant to a fifteen-year-old that Thoreau went to Walden Pond?

Is it possible not to think?

Write of a logic that many people miss.

Discuss self-education.

"Another teacher beat up in school," says a cartoon—"a new philosophy has been added: spare the rod and spoil the teacher." Discuss this condition.

Does a university degree assure the graduate of a better life?

At what age do we first become aware of ourselves and others?

Should high schools require proficiency tests for graduation? How do such tests work in schools where they are already used?

A cartoon says that a modern problem of education is that often the student cannot read his report card. Discuss this condition.

What ought a summer program at a university to be like?

How much do college graduates know about their fields?

Discuss this quotation by Sir Francis Bacon, "I have taken all knowledge as my province."

Write a paper about "After-Maths"—higher math, etc.

What unconscious research does the mind make?

Write on the revival of _____.

Emerson said that life consists in what one is thinking all day. Discuss.

What new policies exist for grading papers?

What new teaching trends are there, either in pedagogy or subject matter?

What are the responsibilities of students in high school?

Develop the thesis: "_____ is an education."

What besides the mind and soul is educable?

What will your child's first teacher expect of him/her?

Give "Some Advice and Some Instructions" concerning education.

"He is wise who learns from everyone," says a proverb. Discuss.

Write on self-improvement.

Discuss John Donne's words, "Go, and catch a falling star . . ."

Why is the college presidency such a difficult profession?

Discuss low/high brainpower.

Discuss opening up new worlds in education.

Discuss learning all the angles of _____.

Discuss a significant discovery about _____.

What did Helen Keller say she would concentrate on seeing if given only three days to see? Discuss her answer as it concerns you.

Judge the employment outlook over the next ten years in different areas of teaching.

One Out of Every Five Grownups in the United States Functionally Illiterate, says a headline. Discuss this condition.

What should be the function(s) of an educator?

Discuss University admissions policies.

What is a data bank, and how does it work?

Law

Is *all* punishment "cruel and unusual"?

Discuss legal probes on television.

Discuss first offenders and the law.

"The age of chivalry is never past," said Kingsley, "so long as there is a wrong left unredressed on earth." Discuss.

Discuss abuses by miltary cadre.

Discuss illegal drugs in high school.

Discuss "the law's delay" (*Hamlet*).

Discuss how one can legally fight the boss.

Regarding a lien on an apartment or on an automobile, what is exempt from the law?

Are there any uniform prison/jail standards?

How do natural-disaster victims appeal for government-assistance funds?

How is the legal system being called upon to judge mother against father, one lifestyle against another?

What are some unusual legal or insurance services?

In Houston, Texas, there are thieves of, of all things, grease—especially cooking grease left outside restaurants for pickup. What theft of other unusual things do you know of?

Do research, and then write on, the question of who owns the mailbox legally. Does the government own it, or does the person whose mail is directed to it? What restrictions and so forth are there on and for mailboxes?

Is hijacking the "real Bermuda Triangle," as one newspaper has said?

What is prison life like in Argentina?

What are some typical laws about posters—kinds of posters, kinds of display, and so forth?

How can one legally protect his/her job?

Where does the court stand on obscenity?

What ordinances about pornography exist at the small-town level?

Do military or political bodies in the United States have a record of "dealing with" people who threaten to blow the whistle on them?

Show how "Muzak" has tried to deal with bank robberies.

Write about the pickpocket conditions of a certain area.

Discuss the law about racial-ethnic listings or identifications.

What ways does the law provide for allowing someone to get off the hook?

Discuss personal property and the law.

Tell what it was like during the 1950s Red Hunt in the United States.

Discuss violent encounters outside the law.

Discuss mail fraud.

Discuss counterfeit documents—passports, visas, recommendations, birth certificates, graduation certificates, university transcripts, and so forth.

Discuss the law and the right to protect news sources.

What does the law do about rape?

What does the law do statistically about burglaries?

What are some legal abuses by the FBI?

Discuss law and the "frame."

Discuss cracking down on _____.

Discuss the comeback(s) of blacklisted writers.

Discuss consumer protection and the law.

Discuss solitary confinement and the law.

Can students collect legal damages from their schools?

What are your rights concerning the pledge of allegiance?

Considered from the legal side, does our patent system work?

Argentina Requires Religious Registration, says a headline. Discuss.

Discuss Mafia control of the law and government.

Discuss witness protection under the law. What does the law do about threats?

Discuss "The Great American Fraud."

Discuss the rash of thefts of small airplanes.

Discuss the law and bribery.

Discuss justice in _____.

Discuss computer crimes—telephone calls made free, misuse of bank credit cards, illegal bank withdrawals, and so forth.

Travel, Transportation

Write of a "lifetime" car.

Do auto makers put profits ahead of lives?

Discuss long-distance car travel.

Airbus Newest Plane Entry into Aviation Controversy, says a Jack Anderson headline. Discuss.

Discuss modern ways of improving cars for luxury or comfort.

Discuss modern ways of improving cars for safety.

What difficulties would one encounter in taking a car into a foreign country?

Discuss bicycle speed barriers.

Discuss four-wheel-drive vehicles.

Discuss road discipline.

Discuss "the parking-space neurosis" (Art Buchwald).

Discuss American driving.

Animals, Plants, Natural Phenomena

Discuss the "animals nobody loves"—rattlesnake, coyote, and wild mustang.

Discuss the illegal use of contaminated animals for food.

Discuss the abuse of animals.

Discuss cat personality.

Discuss pet cemeteries.

Discuss the intelligence of animals.

How do elephants establish graveyards?

Do animals have their own territory?

Discuss animals and language.

Discuss animals and neurosis.

Discuss the habits and characteristics of kangaroos.

What does it mean that the mother mink sets out five food settings for her five children?

Are sharks as dangerous as *Jaws* showed?

Discuss ostrich ranching.

Do we have anything to fear from birds?

Fleas Dine on People in South Florida, says a headline. Discuss.

What is the truth about the black widow spider?

What is the ant king of the world?

Can anything be gained by talking to plants?

Discuss hunting for truffles.

Discuss the ecosphere, the area from which our natural resources (everything needed to support life, in this case) come.

Discuss the control of forest fires.

What should plants be fed?

Discuss desert agriculture.

Discuss Siberian resources.

What is the value of a swamp?

Do we know what electricity is?

Discuss the "challenge of the deep."

Discuss the fact that Europe and America were once part of the same land.

Discuss the role of the laser in the future.

Consider the ramifications of the Law of Entropy—the theory that the universe has reached its peak and is winding down.

Religion, Beliefs

What did early human beings believe that we now do not believe?

Discuss the fact that it has been argued by some that Jesus came to the American continent; that ancient prophets foresaw the Columbus expeditions.

What is involved in spiritual freedom?

Investigate what is meant by the fact that the Vatican may release the Jewish catacombs.

What are some current religious problems?

What are some religious myths that ought to be eliminated?

What are some religious questions that are unsettled?

Discuss some intimations of mortality/immortality.

Discuss the belief that there are ghosts that don't know what happened to them, that don't know, for example, that they are ghosts or how they died.

Discuss black magic of ancient times.

Discuss black magic of modern times.

What is the role of the Bible in our national life?

Write about the snake handlers, an American religious sect.

Write about new religions associated with Christianity.

Write about new religions not associated with Christianity.

Write about the expansion of religion into television.

Write about the growing relationship between religion and politics.

The Media, Rhetoric, Communication

Is pleasure the first attraction of writing?

Discuss propaganda and elections.

Do kids listen to the words of popular music?

How offensive can television get?

Does the newspaper concern itself with news?

How can the audience affect programing on television?

Write about the (imagined) results of a newspaper recipe that had several mistakes in it, say, with the ingredients and the measures.

If people were taped so that they knew what they sound like, would they change in their speech habits or their behavior?

Write of any entertainment (book, movie, play, TV show, etc.) that wanders aimlessly, without purpose.

What are some reasons movie producers have for delaying the release of their films?

Discuss a famous composer-lyricist team.

How is TV used in the field of medicine?

How does TV present useful information in an interesting way?

If actors pursue a second career in the media, what is it usually? Why?

How can questionable taste in TV be made more palatable?

What is a "real" person in fiction?

How is a symphony like a play?

Should news reporters be entertainers?

How are unfair ads removed by law from TV or radio?

Write of a campaign waged against a certain advertisement or against certain kinds of advertisements.

Do the children of stars almost always experience neglect along with luxury?

How might a writer's characters come to gain control of the writer?

What do we mean when we say that a certain TV show is "predictable"?

Discuss the changing shape of television.

The producers of certain bilingual programs for children are aiming for "a generation without cultural hang-ups." Discuss.

Write on legal language.

In what ways have certan futuristic novels (such as Huxley's *Brave New World* and Orwell's *1984*) proved themselves to have been accurate forecasts?

Write on a certain theory of meaning.

Write on the loss of important records.

Write on certain word traps associated with the media.

Write on TV and censorship.

Tell what the Burma Shave commercials (or other past American folklore items in advertisements) were like.

Is *any* second language hard for anyone who comes to it for the first time?

Write on bumper stickers as American dialogue.

Where has censorship arrived if book-burners have banned a Bobbsey Twins book?

Write on editorial cartoons.

Write on ESP.

Write on bleeping as a new way of life in America.

Is the American public reading more, or less?

How accurate are newspapers as keepers of history?

How accurate are historians as keepers of history?

"The strength of a community comes from the ability and desire of its people to communicate with one another," a newspaper item says. Discuss.

The printed word means everything in Washington, Art Buchwald observes. Discuss.

Write on propaganda in Soviet life.

Write on censorship in a foreign country.

Write on censorship in advertising.

What is the translator's greatest problem?

What is the language of schizophrenia?

Write on the battle for possession of the mind—through radio, television, books, religion, and so forth.

A cartoon asks whether government will have to set up a Department of Paperwork to get rid of paperwork in government. Discuss.

Do newspapers have good world reportage?

What should be the role of television and of newspapers?

Write of a program in which business executives are learning how to speak, write, and read.

Write of talking books for the blind.

Write an essay in salute to and in memory of radio.

Is bad usage of language contagious?

Write on the growing importance of English as a commercial language of the world.

Write on the lost art of direct expression.

Are there any good, or even admirable, advertisements?

Will Americans be the death of English?

How might the author of a classic from the last century react to today's analysis of the book?

Write on over-correctness or pseudo-correctness.

Write on the government and television.

Write on exchanges of favors among television networks.

Write on the new trend in advertising, in which there are direct attacks on opposing commercial products.

Write on what television advertisers and television producers do to avoid unfortunate juxtaposition between products and shows.

What are some important misconceptions about language?

Does anyone read our greatest books?

What do people write to the editor of the newspaper?

Newsmen Guilty of Felonious Assaults on the Language, says *TV Guide*. Discuss.

Do Americans prefer plain talk to the cliché?

Do words often conceal more than they express?

LBJ was conned into giving a pep talk to the wrong troops, so that he addressed returning troops as if they were troops destined for Vietnam. Discuss.

Do editors read and heed letters to the editor?

Health, Medicine

Write of someone who has regained eyesight after blindness.

Write of required drug warnings.

Write of hobbies for health.

Write of the link between the mind and the body.

Write of research into cures for cancer.

Write of control of VD.

Write on food poisoning.

Write on allergies in the home.

Is medical science now equipped to deal with any disease?

Write on the common cold.

Write on fallout and health.

Write on medical uses of plants and herbs.

Write on some biological hazard.

Safe Nuclear Burial Unlikely: Geologists, says a headline. Discuss.

Write on the bubonic plague of modern times.

Write on feeding by vein.

Write on the special medical unit associated with police departments.

Write on carbon monoxide poisoning.

Is there anything that can be done to protect public water from being sabotaged?

How can one play it safe with drinking water?

How has plastic surgery for veterans been practiced with great success?

What are some complications of pregnancy?

What are operational problems of a veterans' hospital?

What new directions have been taken in epidemiology?

What does Aristotle observe about sleep and sleeplessness?

Write on wheezing and sneezing.

How do pockets of air beneath the water save lives?

Politics, Government, History

Write of someone who was immensely successful in a first venture at politics.

How does the Soviet government put down dissidents?

Write on the erosion of freedom in democratic states.

Can freedom be too much for many people to handle, as it has been said?

Write an essay, "Two Cheers for _____."

How is an aristocrat trained for rule?

Write an attack on a certain political group. Write of an attack that has been made on a certain political group.

The cartoon Blondie says that politicians who promise to put petunia beds in every park do not exactly stick their necks out. Discuss.

Human Rights Uproar Has Ignored Cambodia, says a Jack Anderson headline. Discuss.

How do secret organizations work to put down those against them?—this question re Dick Gregory's accusation that the FBI told the Mafia he had criticized them.

Discuss a politician's saying, "If you vote for me, the rains will come!"

Discuss the passing of the cavalry.

How accurate is history as it is portrayed on the screen?

Discuss immigration (or emigration) policies.

What goes on in the army that the army would prefer the public not know?

Write on political sloganry.

Write on the transition from one president to the next.

Write on Democracy and "Democracy."

Write on the bureaucratic use of government vehicles and other items.

How popular is the royal family of Great Britain?

Write on White House news conferences.

Summarize a certain public figure's position on a certain issue—amnesty, inflation, the Panama Canal, for example.

What is life in Washington, D.C. like?

What are the vital functions of the United States Census Bureau?

Write on government in the banana republics.

Write on island-hopping during World War II.

What crises play big parts in elections?

Write on prisoner exchanges or spy exchanges.

Can *anyone* run for political office?

How is it argued that J. Edgar Hoover covered his tracks?

Explain the Teapot Dome Scandal.

What was the last blow to the South in the American Civil War?

What usually happens in off-year elections?

Write on the concept of global responsibility.

Write of minority representation in American government.

Write of foreign influence on American governmental decisions.

Why did a certain Japanese admiral say, "We have waked a sleeping giant"?

Why is the British government not enforcing the metric switch?

What part does celebrity status play in politics?

Write about alive history in _____ (Williamsburg, St. Augustine, etc.).

Write of some issue having to do with territorial rights.

What happened at Babi Yar?

What procedure is behind a presidential decision?

Write of so-called "instant history"—bringing the pyramids, bridges, and so forth of the famous past to the United States.

Write on this quotation from Bill Moyers: "Most presidents don't rise above their times. They reflect their times."

The columnist Andy Rooney wants "a candidate who dreams big and then sets out to make the dream come true." Write of such a candidate that you know of.

ARGUMENTATION

What Argumentation Is

In its root sense, argumentation musters proof and brings it forth in order to persuade, defend, or, at times, attack. In that stricter sense this process of writing is logical and formal. Let us free the term from its dictionary sense and let it come to grips with anything from a legal brief to a political donnybrook. Exposition fights to explain, argumentation to win.

How to Write Argumentation

Once again, clarity is essential as with any kind of writing. We emphasize it again here because argument so often tends to become melded with emotion. Even if argumentative material demands a certain degree of ambiguity or subjectiveness, the one who argues should be clear about it. The word "argue" is akin to "argent," which meant "silver" in its archaic usage, "whiteness" otherwise, and in either case suggests clarifying or purifying through refinement. The reader—especially the one who is likely to disagree with the writer to begin with—will chuck every impurity back at the writer. There would be nothing unpalatable to spit out in an ideal argument so clear that the reader would have to swallow it.

A balanced, reasonable approach is often most effective, and it is always better to gather more proof than opinion. Nothing is more likely to put people off than a hedgehog piece of writing bristling with opinions. Reason and logic are not the end-all of anything, however, though we sometimes find it comforting to believe they might be. Emotion is powerful; it has moved nations. But emotional appeals are skittish. They tend to bolt off the track. Riding them rhetorically is dangerous even for experienced writers. Anyone attempting to argue from emotion should remember that the faster the heart races, the tighter the rein.

It can be instructive simply to argue a position for the fun of it, to play the devil's advocate. But when you turn serious about it and are out to win the day you had best believe in what you are doing. Be sincere. Sincerity convinces. It will help you see clearly through the thick of things. Anything else will work against you. Truth persists between the lines of a hypocritical page like checked light through a lattice.

Integrity, then, is the place where you make your stand. Imagination can broaden the field. Reason, logic, emotion, humor, irony, satire—any of these can be viable forms of argumentation. How you use them is another matter. You might find yourself brandishing a polemical club. (Writing polemically is often looked down upon in this age of media hype, but it is well to remember that in his own day Milton was probably better known for his pamphleteering than for his poetry.) Or is it an irenic olive branch you brush across the page? Then maybe you turn acrobat, tumble your argument on its grinning head, much as Swift did when he made his modest proposal. Circumstance will have its say. Only stand firmly in the integrity of your argument.

Locating Subjects for Argumentation

Argumentation is another substantial section of this book. Almost anything can become controversial, including most of the subjects listed in this book. A word of caution, though, before this chapter is crossed with other disciplines and techniques: It is best to keep forms and priorities straight. Creative writing, for example, is, generally speaking, ill suited for the purpose of argumentation. Powerful arguments can be made creatively, but the difference between argumentation and art is definitive.

62

--------Taken from <u>What Can I Write About? 7000 Topics for High School Students</u> by David Powell

Education, Learning, Experience

What ought to be the rules for bilingual education?

Why should we read "that old stuff"?

What ought the university to demand of its students?

Where should college and university costs be cut?

Where should be the limits of aid for schools?

Is it criminal to omit to teach?

Is there too much (or is there not enough) hair-splitting in education?

Which is it better to see: the forest, or the trees?

Agree/disagree: There are some who see neither the forest nor the trees.

What is the place of, or what should be the place of, the scholar in public life?

What debt does education owe to the past?

Argue for/against functional-literacy tests.

Argue for/against travel as education.

Argue for/against Samuel Johnson's opinion, "The Giant's Causeway is worth seeing, but not worth going to see." In other words, argue whether it is best to go out of your way to see something, or to see it only incidentally.

Argue for/against proliferation in education.

Argue for/against easy A's or the profusion of A's.

Argue for/against letter grades.

Argue for/against allowing students (especially young children) to choose for themselves among educational alternatives.

Agree/disagree: "A little learning is a dangerous thing." —Pope.

Agree/disagree with John Dewey's opinion about the purpose of the university.

Agree/disagree with Cardinal Newman's opinion about the purpose of the university.

Agree/disagree: "The modern university is the survival of everyone, the failure of no one."

Agree/disagree with the argument that politicians and bureaucrats should be required to take literacy tests.

Agree/disagree with the time-arrangement for your school year.

Agree/disagree: Teaching has failed.

Agree/disagree: There are too many restrictions on teaching.

Agree/disagree: There are not enough restrictions on students.

Agree/disagree: National tests should be changed so that they do not probe psyches but instead probe knowledge and the use of knowledge.

Agree/disagree: There is too much time off among students for special activities.

Argue for/against school prayers.

Argue for/against sex education.

Argue for/against teacher strikes.

Argue for/against private schools.

Argue for/against books.

Argue for/against censorship of certain kinds of books.

Argue for/against letting the student teach other students.

Argue for/against open discipline by teachers.

Argue for/against a certain change in the curriculum.

Argue for/against a university education.

Argue for/against periodically grading teachers on their subjects.

Argue for/against fraternities/sororities.

Argue for/against student government.

Argue for/against strictness of form in school work.

Argue for/against precision in word choice and spelling.

Argue for/against co-education.

Argue for/against busing of students to promote integration.

Argue for/against setting a personal goal early in life.

Argue for/against parental direction in determining children's careers.

Argue for/against high registration fees.

Argue for/against playing soft music during examinations.

Who ought to be permitted to serve on the school board?

Who ought to have the responsibility (and authority) for educational policy?

What is the limit, if any, of academic freedom?

On what should one be graded: performance, or ability?

Agree/disagree: "We live, increasingly, in a society in which poor students are not flunked, and bad workers cannot be fired. We should not wonder that we are drowning in shoddiness." (George Will)

Agree/disagree: It is possible to be an expert in many things nowadays.

Discuss argumentatively, and in terms of experience: "The most interesting things are those that didn't occur."

Discuss argumentatively, and in terms of experience: The author of *Genesis* had "no conception of the stars." (Clarence Darrow)

Agree/disagree: Sometimes children misbehave because they want to be corrected.

Argue for/against being young again.

Argue for/against spanking.

Argue for/against adolescent freedom.

Discuss argumentatively whether there is anything not yet done that is worth doing.

Agree/disagree: "Human kind cannot bear very much reality."—T. S. Eliot

Does American history as it is taught in school tell the truth?

Does science as it is taught in school tell the truth?

Agree/disagree: "Christmas comes too early."

Agree/disagree: "There's nothing wrong with sameness."

Agree/disagree: "It is easier to be reasonable than unreasonable."

Agree/disagree: Solitude is one of the happiest routes to happiness.

Agree/disagree: Solitude is one of our best teachers.

Agree/disagree with the opinion about experience that good is not always rewarded and evil is not always punished.

In growing up, *does* Hope remain supreme, or does it not even reign at all?

Agree/disagree, with regards to education and experience: "Damn braces. Bless relaxes."—William Blake

Does philosophy have a real place in the world? Should it occupy as important a place as it does in educating us?

Should everyone be admitted to the university? Should there be no restrictions on entry?

Agree/disagree: The microcomputer in education is a passing fad.

Agree/disagree that students should be allowed to sue schools for wrongly educating them.

What should be taught?

What should not be taught?

Argue for/against federal spending for education.

Argue for/against student employment as an education or important experience.

Argue for/against the function of the university as a giver of moral education.

What modern songwriter's songs could be fruitfully studied in school?

Agree/disagree with the opinion of Henry, Baron Brougham: "Education makes a people easy to lead, but difficult to drive; easy to govern, but impossible to enslave."

According to Sir Francis Bacon, what, why, and how ought we to read? Agree/disagree with his statement.

Should students be paid as an encouragement for them to attend school?

What knowledge is needed before all other knowledge?

Agree/disagree: Teachers should enliven their classes with entertainment.

Discuss argumentatively any *modern* book which educated and changed the world.

Argue a particular way in which textbooks should be chosen.

Argue the point whether near-misses teach anything.

Is it true that "what is asserted without proof may be denied without proof"?

Argue what truth is and where to find it.

Argue for a civics class syllabus as *you* would teach it.

Agree/disagree with the opinion that knowledge can get in the way.

Does what we don't know hurt us?

What, if anything, should be done about absenteeism in school?

Is it true that, as novelist John Gardner has said, our schools are "thrown up like barricades in the way of young minds"? Does school education thwart, or does it assist, life education?

Discuss argumentatively Edna St. Vincent Millay's poetic statement, "And he whose soul is flat—the sky/Will cave in on him by and by."

Discuss argumentatively T. S. Eliot's poetic statement, "Teach us to care and not to care./Teach us to sit still."

Discuss argumentatively Max Beerbohm's statement, "The Socratic manner is not a game at which two can play."

Discuss argumentatively Emerson's statement, "A foolish consistency is the hobgoblin of little minds."

Discuss argumentatively Browning's statement, "Burrow awhile and build, broad on the roots of things."

Discuss argumentatively the statement by Sinclair Lewis, "We are coming out . . . of the stuffiness of safe, sane, and incredibly dull provincialism."

Discuss argumentatively: "A worthy idea is one that withstands resistance."

Agree/disagree with Thoreau's argument that it is not necessary to travel in order to learn.

Discuss argumentatively: "A popular government, without popular information or the means of acquiring it, is but a prologue to a farce or a tragedy or perhaps both. Knowledge will forever govern ignorance, and a people who mean to be their own governors must arm themselves with the power which knowledge gives." (James Madison)

Discuss argumentatively Sir Francis Bacon's statement, "Silence is the virtue of fools."

Discuss argumentatively Sir Thomas Browne's statement, "We carry within us the wonders we seek without us."

Discuss argumentatively Thomas Henry Huxley's statement, "Irrationally held truths may be more harmful than reasoned errors."

Discuss argumentatively Ezra Pound's statement, "It was you that broke the new wood,/Now is a time for carving."

Argue for/against any of the following schools: Harvard, Yale, Stanford, West Point.

Agree/disagree: "Still water runs deep." (Does it run at all, by the way?)

Agree/disagree with the argument that grades indicate something about achievement.

How can it be that, as John Donne said, "affliction is a treasure"?

Argue a particular formula or standard for judging when a person is educated. Argue the evaluation of your education.

Argue the point whether it is fun to have to work in order to know.

Argue whether there should be less rhetoric and more action in teaching.

Argue what the best lesson is that education gives.

Argue whether history is "bunk."

Argue for/against reading *only* for pleasure.

Argue for/against the opinion that there is too much learning and too little common sense.

Argue for/against the junior college or community college.

Argue for/against some procedure at a junior college or a community college.

What questions are there that might be asked but shouldn't be answered?

Argue for/against the opinion that the reach of the imagination is infinite.

Argue for/against the opinion that teachers have enough time to teach.

Argue for/against the opinion that the term "unknown quantity" can be used in some academic discipline other than science or mathematics.

Argue for/against the opinion that people are what they observe and absorb.

Law

Argue for/against open meetings.

Argue what should be done about spouse abuse.

Agree/disagree with Tolstoy's statement, "All are guilty; none is innocent."

Agree/disagree: Everyone breaks the law.

Argue what should be done under the law about noise pollution.

Argue what should be done under the law to regulate charity organizations.

Argue for/against lie-detector tests.

What should be done under the law about chain letters?

What law(s) should be created for certain new ways of life?

Argue for/against "privilege under law."

What old laws, if any, should be re-instituted?

Argue for/against some general position the law takes.

What can be done, or what should be done, to a biased or prejudiced judge?

Argue for/against the opinion that criminals profit from counsel.

Argue for/against the 55 mph speed limit.

Argue what ought to be done about drugs.

Argue what ought to be done about drug pushers.

Who ought to be, or who ought not to be, arrested?

Argue the point whether anything gets done under the law from radical positions.

Agree/disagree: The father of a child is not always known; the mother is—so why should not the mother's last name be used for children?

Argue for/against adoption by single parents.

Argue what parental responsibility is under the law.

Argue whether it depends on the individual to say what is good and what is bad.

What should the law be concerning censorship?

What should be done to protect patients in nursing homes?

What ought to be done under the law about stray animals?

Argue for/against abortion as considered under the law.

Argue for/against a certain hunting or fishing law.

Argue for/against the contention that in law it is best to act alone in defense of oneself.

Argue for/against a law requiring parents to leave a legacy for their children.

Argue for/against the argument that there ought to be a way to earn special privileges under the law.

Argue for/against unmarked police cars.

Argue for/against ambulance hustlers.

Argue for/against minor offenses being legally treated as major ones.

Argue for/against major offenses being legally treated as minor ones.

Argue for/against treating adolescents as adults are treated under the law.

Argue for/against a certain light sentence or heavy sentence handed down.

Argue what ought to be legally done to punish a foreign nation that has committed a crime against the United States.

Argue for/against questioning the judge.

Argue for/against courtroom television.

Argue for/against the jury system as it is.

Argue the point whether illegal acts by a president are excusable.

Argue what ought to be done with the accused who await trial.

Argue what you would do if your friend broke a serious law.

Argue whether violent acts in self-defense are defensible.

Argue for/against certain parking laws.

Argue for/against FBI raids without recourse by the persons raided.

Argue for/against easing a certain ban.

Argue for/against the contention that there ought to be unanimity among jurors in their verdicts.

Argue for/against oaths of loyalty.

Argue for/against subliminal advertising.

Argue for/against electronic eavesdropping.

Argue for/against smoking in public places.

Argue for/against the conscience as law.

Argue for/against no-fault insurance.

Argue for/against change of venue (generally or in specific cases).

Argue for/against a catchall law—that is, one that covers many things at one time.

What ought to be done under the law about antitrust violations?

What standards ought there to be for medical suits?

What safety codes ought there to be for traffic chases, ambulances, and so forth?

Argue for/against cracking down on jaywalkers.

Argue for/against the right to die.

Argue for/against gun control.

Argue for/against being required to serve on a jury.

Argue whether heroin should be legally used as a pain-killer.

Argue whether actors should be legally responsible for claims they make for the products they endorse.

Argue whether it is so that, as George Halifax said, "Men are not hanged for stealing horses, but that horses may not be stolen."

Who ought to be responsible for paying for a window broken by a child under fifteen?

What laws ought there to be about kidnapping?

What standards ought there to be for legal remunerative awards?

What laws are there, or what laws ought there to be, to protect innocent bystanders?

Discuss argumentatively Thomas Drummond's statement, "Property has its duties as well as its rights."

Argue whether drivers should be regularly retested.

Argue whether there should be a maximum age for drivers.

Argue whether a stock marketer should be considered (for tax purposes, let us say) a legal gambler.

What laws ought there to be to protect privacy?

What laws ought there to be to protect confidentiality?

What laws ought there to be to protect workers from their bosses?

What laws ought there to be to protect bosses from their workers?

Discuss argumentatively Edmund Burke's statement, "There is a limit at which forbearance ceases to be a virtue."

Discuss argumentatively W. H. Auden's comment, "Thou shalt not sit with statisticians nor commit a social science."

Argue for/against capital punishment as seen *only* from the concept of justice.

Argue for/against a certain pardon.

Argue for/against a certain extradition.

Argue for/against minding your own business (as regards the law).

Argue for/against the de-emphasis of a certain law.

Argue what the rights of children ought to be under the law.

Who, legally considered, should/should not be allowed to drive?

Argue for/against the stricter enforcement of traffic laws.

Should political lying be considered a crime?

Argue for/against the measure-for-measure, eye-for-an-eye law.

Should those who make war be the only ones who have to fight it?

Argue for/against the position that the self is private property.

Argue for/against putting capital punishment on national television.

Argue for/against standing alone for what we believe in, and without help.

What ought to be the law for protecting private citizens against harassment by government officials?

Discuss John Locke's statement, "The end of the law is, not to abolish or restrain, but to preserve and enlarge freedom."

Argue for/against a law that restricts freedom.

Argue for/against absolute free speech.

Argue for/against the right of bigots to be heard, to be read, to march, to protest.

Argue for/against a certain legality concerning athletics.

Agree/disagree: "No one has the right to destroy the land one owns."

Can (and should) punishment always "fit the crime"?

Write an argumentative essay about the law entitled, "What's Yours Isn't Mine."

Argue for/against certain general practices of lawyers. What ought lawyers to do in order to shape up?

What ought to be done to protect people from being indiscriminately committed to insane asylums?

What ought to be done about property taxes?

What should be the punishment for second offenders? for first offenders?

What qualifications ought to exist for a police chief?

What qualifications ought to exist for a trial judge?

What argumentative position does some sacred book (Bible, Talmud, or Koran, for example) take on some public questions such as capital punishment, abortion, pacifism, and so forth?

Who has the right of way?

We reserve the right to _____.

What recourse under the law is there for _____? What recourse ought there to be?

Argue for/against the position that Bingo is a form of legal gambling.

Discuss argumentatively Walter Van Tilburg Clark's statement, "A mob is no more intelligent than its least intelligent member."

Discuss argumentatively the right to remain silent and not reveal the source of certain information.

Discuss argumentatively the headline, Escapee Sues Jailers for Allowing Him to Break Out.

Interpret argumentatively a single passage of the United States Constitution regarding elections, immigration, personal rights, gun laws, and so forth.

Argue who ought to have immunity in politics, medicine, law, religion.

Argue the point who owns space.

Argue the point who owns the seas.

Argue the point whether grand juries further justice, or hinder it.

Argue whether there was obstruction of justice at Kent State.

Argue what should be done under the law with terrorists when they are captured.

Look into the local laws and see which of them ought to be obsolete.

Should Stalin be tried, at least for the record, for murder?

Argue who can be legally excluded from being given financial credit.

Argue for/against the position taken by Emperor Ferdinand I, "Let justice be done, though the world perish."

Discuss argumentatively a Southern Illinois Group that tried to have power to investigate foreigners and to institute university dress codes.

Accidents caused by drunk drivers are not involuntary, it has been said; the argument is that the drivers *want* to drink and therefore should be responsible for their volution. Discuss this point argumentatively.

What should be a telephone law?

Discuss argumentatively the Blue Laws, especially with regard to such contradictions in them as that someone can buy beer on Sunday but not ice.

Discuss argumentatively this newspaper quotation: "A Roman Catholic bishop says restoration of the death penalty is 'counterproductive to the pro-life crusade of the church'."

Should one be required to stand up during the national anthem?

Write an argumentative essay entitled, "Which Is Better, Military Justice or Civilian Justice?"

Discuss argumentatively the fact that France still uses the guillotine for execution, though a bill has been sent to the French Senate to abolish it.

Argue for/against the Biblical injunction, "Judge not, that you be not judged."

Discuss argumentatively the fact that a certain paint-sniffer said he sniffed paint because God gave it to sniff.

Discuss argumentatively alcoholism and the law.

Discuss argumentatively whether citizens need more police protection during strikes.

Discuss argumentatively a Jeffrey Hart column whose headline reads, "Sacco and Vanzetti Memorial Nothing But Political Freak-Out."

Government, Politics

Should proceedings of office holders be televised?

Argue for/against rule by aristocracy.

Argue for/against MacArthur's firing by Truman.

Argue some point having to do with local or regional interests.

What should be the restrictions on public funds used by politicians?

Argue for/against Ayn Rand's position(s) as stated in her books.

Discuss argumentatively, and concerning government, Thomas Gray's statement, "A favorite has no friend."

Agree/disagree: "The world needs troublemakers."

Agree or disagree with the opinion that the Nixon-Frost interviews were useful.

Agree or disagree with the opinion that Sir Thomas More was the admirable person that popular history says he was.

Agree/disagree: "The great man cannot be overly cautious."

Argue for/against a certain position taken by a president.

Argue what a recent poll proves.

Agree or disagree with the opinion that the United States should make a certain reparation.

Argue whether a power structure prevails in the United States government.

Argue whether Puerto Rico should be made a state in the United States.

Argue what the United States can do to control treatment of foreign peoples in their countries.

Discuss argumentatively John Fletcher's statement, "Let the world slide."

Argue whether the United States is prepared for _____ .

Argue how the United States might prepare for _____ .

Argue for/against keeping things the way they are in _____ .

Argue for/against the premise of a certain movie on politics or government.

Argue for/against political or financial controls of newspapers.

Argue for/against shaking up the system.

Argue for/against write-in ballots.

Argue for/against a political watchdog program.

Argue for/against warrantless activities by the government.

Argue for/against government materials/premises/promises.

Argue for/against youthful people in high political places.

Argue for/against the very old in high political places.

Agree/disagree: "Something for everyone is nothing for anyone."

Argue for/against a top-heavy government.

Discuss Walt Whitman's statement, "The United States themselves are essentially the greatest poem."

Discuss whether our foreign policy is in a shambles.

Agree/disagree: "There are too many people—and consequently there is too much confusion—in Civil Service."

Agree/disagree: "Only in America do we pretend to worship the majority, reverently listening to the herd as it Gallups this way and that." (Gore Vidal)

Argue for/against military government.

Argue for/against: "The government should be responsible for toxic-waste problems."

Argue for/against a political individual who is generally considered radical.

Argue for/against the Peace Corps or some other such peripheral body of the government.

Argue for/against the opinion of Samuel Johnson, "Patriotism is the last refuge of a scoundrel."

Argue for/against revealing government secrets.

Argue for/against the opinion of Samuel Johnson, "He who praises everybody praises nobody."

Argue for/against the opinion of John Dryden, "Better one suffer, than a nation grieve."

"The king never dies," said Sir William Blackstone. Argue whether the President of the United States ever dies.

Argue for/against a United States Parliament.

Argue for/against the Constitution.

Discuss argumentatively the contention by Charles James Fox that "The right of governing is a trust, not a property."

Discuss argumentatively the statement by Thomas Jefferson, "No duty the Executive had to perform was so trying as to put the right man in the right place."

Discuss argumentatively the opinion that those who are behind the president are the ones who really ought to be watched carefully.

Discuss argumentatively the opinion of Samuel Johnson that "Most schemes of political improvement are very laughable things."

Argue for/against a modest government proposal.

Argue for/against certain political appointments instead of elections.

Argue for/against a minority figure for president.

Just to sharpen your argumentative skills, argue *against* voting.

Argue a certain appointment that the president ought to make.

Discuss argumentatively Henrik Ibsen's quotation (from one of his play characters): "The minority is always right."

Argue what you can do when you disagree with the government.

Argue what the postal service can do to come out even, or perhaps even make money.

Agree/disagree with the opinion that we need political heroes today.

Discuss argumentatively this quotation from Thomas Jefferson: "When a man assumes a public trust, he should consider himself a public property."

Discuss argumentatively this quotation from Robert Frost: "Good fences make good neighbors."

Discuss argumentatively the opinion that the state is the greatest danger to the well-being of humanity.

Discuss argumentatively how we can pay back the founders of the nation.

Discuss argumentatively what fight ought to be waged over America's future.

Discuss argumentatively what should be the prime target of government reform.

Discuss argumentatively how you can bully the government.

Discuss argumentatively whether nice guys finish last in politics.

Discuss argumentatively this quotation from George Halifax: "To the question, What shall we do to be saved in this world? there is no other answer but this, Look to your Moat."

Argue whether it is reasonable to think that people don't really want bureaucracies to end.

What would make a draft of _____ necessary or desirable for 19__?

Discuss argumentatively the Spanish proverb, "The monkey dressed in silk is still a monkey."

Argue whether statesmen are born great, or whether they rise to greatness.

Argue whether only the "bad guys" win in politics.

Argue what the government can do to help those without food.

Discuss argumentatively the statement by William Ralph Inge, "Democracy is only an experiment in government, and it has the obvious disadvantage of merely counting votes instead of weighing them."

Discuss argumentatively the statement by Robert Frost, "Something there is that doesn't love a wall."

Argue whether government would protect freedom of speech where the people did not insist upon it.

Argue whether the second word of the term "social security" is misleading.

Argue what is an inescapable future for the United States.

Argue whether it is possible to be an Independent in politics.

Is it too difficult to get rid of incompetent civil servants?

Argue whether the American Civil War has been the worst internal event of the United States.

Argue that the announced intentions of the government are different from the demonstrated intentions.

War and Peace, Strife, Violence

Agree/disagree: "The greatest offense against good is to speak evil of it."—William Hazlitt

Discuss argumentatively: "Wild animals never kill for sport."—James Anthony Froude

Discuss argumentatively Thomas Jefferson's saying, "A little rebellion now and then is a good thing."

Discuss argumentatively the quotation from Ibsen's dramatic work, "One shouldn't put on his best trousers to fight for what is right."

Discuss argumentatively the statement by the cartoon character Thumper, "If you can't say anything good about somebody, don't say anything at all."

Argue for/against protesting the protester.

Argue for/against the contention that war is, according to Norman Angell, "the great illusion."

Argue for/against a certain kind of warfare.

Argue which is more threatening to the human race: nuclear war, or ground war.

Argue for/against power.

Argue what is necessary for peace in the Near East.

Argue for/against the neutron bomb.

Argue where the moral responsibility lies for atrocities of war—whether with the political leaders, the military leaders, the enlisted soldiers, the munitions factory employees, the inventors or developers of weaponry, or the people as a whole.

Argue whether TV violence relieves the "dark side" of people. Do people unconsciously need violence through entertainment to displace their own disposition to violence?

Which is worse, pornography or, to quote Tom Wolfe, "pornoviolence"?

Discuss argumentatively the Biblical statement, "The race is not to the swift, nor the battle to the strong."

Argue for/against the loving of one's enemies.

Argue for/against the opinion that the saying should be: "Speak loudly but carry a little stick."

Discuss argumentatively the violence in sports, to include violence in the grandstands among sports spectators.

Discuss argumentatively Thomas Fuller's statement, "It is a silly game where nobody wins."

Discuss argumentatively (but with reference to his obvious irony) George Orwell's statement in 1984: "War is Peace, Freedom is Slavery, Ignorance is Strength."

Discuss argumentatively the Biblical statement, "Let no man's heart fail because of Goliath."

Discuss argumentatively how much enough force is and how much too much force is.

Discuss argumentatively what can most assure national security.

Discuss argumentatively whether the president really has anything to do with "making war."

Discuss argumentatively Richard L. Tobin's statement about television violence: "There is little connection evinced between the use of violence and the suffering such acts [of violence] would inflict in real life."

Discuss argumentatively whether a person—say, a president—should be honored for having changed a position that had been harmful to humanity.

Agree/disagree: Guns are not a step above the clubs of cave people.

Argue what condition is beyond protest.

Argue what the root of all evil is.

Argue whether passive resistance works.

Athletics, Outdoor Activities

Argue for/against challenging the referee's decision.

Argue for/against a certain athlete's retirement.

Argue for/against the calling of a certain play.

Argue for/against the pay of superstar athletes.

Argue for/against social protest by way of athletic events.

Argue for/against the instant replay as arbitrator.

Agree/disagree: In working for perfection in their sports, many athletes practice the wrong things.

Argue for/against the contention that coaches should be given a certain time to produce winning teams.

Agree/disagree: Nobody loses all the time.

Agree/disagree: Nobody wins all the time.

Argue for/against the high or low rating of a certain athlete.

Argue for/against hunting or fishing—or the killing of a particular creature, such as the eagle.

Argue for/against fireworks.

Freedom, Free Will

Discuss argumentatively: "Freedom of the press belongs to the one who owns one."

Discuss argumentatively the opinion of Samuel Johnson, "The will is free, and that's that."

Agree/disagree: "Freedom is survival."

Agree/disagree: "All Americans are free."

Agree/disagree: "The worst frustration of all is getting what you want."

Transportation

Argue for/against the opinion that car buyers usually have to pay too much for extras . . . or have to pay for too many extras.

Argue whether a certain major roadway is correctly designed for smooth transit.

Agree/disagree: Drivers of eighteen-wheelers are a threat to other drivers.

Which is the best moving company?

Argue whether the old cars are as good as they are said to be.

Argue for/against bicycles as replacements for cars in a certain locale.

Argue for/against using a car in New York City.

Argue for/against going back to trains.

Argue for/against seat belts.

Argue what the best outboard motor is.

Argue what the best transport for cargo by land is.

Argue whether public transportation servants are overworked.

Argue what the old _____ had that the new one does not.

Argue what the new _____ has that the old one did not.

Eating, Drinking, Health

Argue for/against exercising.

Argue for/against fasting.

Argue for/against dieting.

Argue for/against a certain diet.

Argue for/against the claims of the health food adherents.

Argue for/against the effectiveness of Vitamin C for controlling colds.

Argue for/against eating vegetables exclusively.

Argue for/against eating meats exclusively.

Argue for/against polluting the air rather than denying the stomach.

Argue what the most useful food is.

Argue how you can get by in a drinking crowd without drinking but without making a big deal about it.

Argue whether there ought to be a law against television commercials that advertise foods children ought not to eat.

Religion, Creation

Argue whether there was a religious purpose in the creation of the world.

Argue for/against the watch-and-watchmaker conception of creation.

Argue for/against doubt, unbelief, or questioning.

Argue whether God is retired, dead, alive and active.

Discuss argumentatively this quotation from John Gardner the novelist: "Religion's chief value is its conservatism: It keeps us in touch with what at least one section of humanity has believed for centuries."

What, in religious terms, is the highest good? the lowest evil?

Is there ever a time, in religious terms, when lying or even hypocrisy is better than truth?

Agree/disagree: Tobacco is "a branch of the sin of drunkenness, which is the root of all sins."—James I of England

When does the censor who is religiously oriented most show sense?

Argue whether there is a paradise on earth.

Medicine, Psychology

Agree/disagree: Sometimes people don't feel well because they don't want to.

Argue what the obligation is of a medical doctor.

Argue for/against faith healing.

Argue for/against medical treatment.

Argue for/against treatment with herbs.

Argue for/against donation of human organs.

Argue for/against natural childbirth.

Agree/disagree: The idea of biofeedback is as ugly as the word itself.

Argue the best way to break a habit harmful to the health.

Argue for/against taking a certain injection or pill.

Argue for/against the reduction of the number of and power of X-rays.

Argue for/against stricter qualifications for the medical doctor.

Discuss argumentatively, and in terms of psychology: "I love to keep work by me: the idea of getting rid of it nearly breaks my heart."—(paraphrased from Jerome Jerome)

Discuss argumentatively, and in terms of psychology: "The existence of ESP cannot be proved."

Discuss argumentatively, and in terms of psychology: "'Deny yourself' is the never-ending song."—Goethe

Discuss argumentatively, and in terms of psychology: Regarding change, "it is often a comfort to shift one's position and be bruised in a new place."

Science and Progress

Argue for/against Lake Nicaragua as the site of a proposed canal.

Argue for/against a sea-level canal.

Argue for/against the theory of _____.

Argue for/against recycling.

Argue for/against catalytic converters.

Argue for/against a new form of, or new source of, energy.

Agree/disagree: "In almost every case, progress takes back what it gives."

Agree/disagree: "Science is spoiling our way of life."

Agree/disagree: "Progress makes us lazy."

Is Congress, as Rooftop O'Toole says, "the opposite of progress"?

Argue for/against the contention that scientists are responsible for their destructive discoveries.

Argue whether science cares about art.

Argue whether art cares about science.

Argue for/against the opinion that the moon has lost its poetic charm because human beings have walked on it.

Agree/disagree: "There is delight in simple things."

Agree/disagree: "Science is more moral than we usually give it credit for."

Argue for/against daylight saving time.

Argue for/against the contention that progress of a material kind holds back, or interferes with, spiritual progress.

Argue the point whether it is possible to argue with (that is, against) scientific facts.

Argue the point whether it is possible to fool Nature.

Language, Communication

Argue for/against practicing public speaking in front of a mirror.

Argue for/against the revival of Latin.

Argue for/against adopting a new trend in public language.

Argue for/against diagraming sentences.

Argue for/against a certain language usage.

Argue for/against prohibition of speaking one's first language when it is the second language of the society.

Agree/disagree: "Not everything—for example, a deep thought or feeling—can be communicated in words."

Agree/disagree: "The corruption of language is the corruption of civilization."

Agree/disagree: "There is nothing sacred about words in print."

Agree/disagree: "One should fear silence."

Agree/disagree: "Silence is golden."

Agree/disagree: "All writing is persuasion."

Agree/disagree: "All language is persuasion."

Agree/disagree: "We speak even in our silences."

Agree/disagree: "Anyone can write, anyone can create."

Agree/disagree: "Black dialect is a language, not a corruption of English."

Agree/disagree: "There is an immense amount of biased listening and inaccurate listening."—(Eric Sevareid, on the occasion of his retirement from CBS television.)

Agree/disagree on the point of whether language sets the tone of civilization.

Agree/disagree with the argument that language does not always mean what it says.

Argue for/against learning to speak Russian, Japanese, Arabic, or some other language not your own.

Argue whether the language of the holy scriptures is the same in any language. Argue whether it is the same, consistently, even in a single language.

Discuss argumentatively the battle over the right to one's own language—Chicano Spanish, for example, or Quebec French.

Agree/disagree: "There are times when good language is bad sense."

Argue when the "Do Not Disturb" sign should be displayed.

Justify the need for one kind of writing (say, contrast) over another (say, description) to convey a certain purpose.

Argue whether docu-dramas are distorted and therefore, as the writer Mark Harris has said, dangerous.

Argue for/against secrecy in a certain matter.

Argue whether television commercials should concentrate on quality rather than on quantity.

Want to Land a Job? You Might Try Lying, says a headline, with the idea that those who tell the truth, or too much of it, on job applications are often not hired. Discuss argumentatively.

Argue for/against the "chairman" title for a woman.

Agree/disagree: "No people or group can be put under one heading."

Argue whether language is interpreted in different ways in a court of law depending on the persons being tried.

Society, Social Interaction

Are robots human beings?

Are you your brother's keeper?

Each for oneself? All for one and one for all?

Argue for/against joining.

Agree/disagree: To remake the world we have to start with ourselves as individuals.

Agree/disagree: Concern for others is concern for self.

Agree/disagree: Nobody gives a toot any more.

Argue what the matter is with you/me/them.

Agree/disagree: "There's a sucker born every minute." —P. T. Barnum

Agree/disagree: Divorcing parents ought to think first of their children.

Agree/disagree: Apologies are usually good only for those who do the apologizing.

Agree/disagree: "There are secrets in all families." —George Farquhar

Argue what our most worthy inheritance is as a society.

Explain argumentatively a certain shift of population that has occurred.

Argue for/against early marriage.

Argue for/against the "money dance" (in which those who attend a wedding reception pin money on the bride's dress).

Argue for/against birthright.

Argue what is reasonable adult or mature behavior in public.

Agree/disagree: "Love at first sight is as common as love at long sight."

Agree/disagree: "You can take people out of the ghetto but you can't take the ghetto out of the people." —Spiro Agnew

Agree/disagree: It is a stereotype that old people are conservative.

Argue whether there is such a phenomenon as "reverse discrimination."

Argue for/against suburbia.

Argue for/against birth control.

Argue for/against being married.

Argue for/against being single.

Agree/disagree: Being a parent does not make one a parent.

Agree/disagree: Every child should be raised by its natural parents.

Argue for/against the small group.

Argue what you should do if you have sudden visitors when you are engaged in some important activity that you do not want to break off.

Argue in what direction one should throw the stone of criticism.

Argue what society needs to cure its ills.

Argue for/against leaving the house.

Agree/disagree: Tradition should be maintained at all costs.

Discuss argumentatively this UPI headline regarding surrogate mothers: Bearing Child for Others Lacks "Rules."

Agree/disagree: A home without a pet is not complete.

Argue some issue of feminism that until now has been completely ignored.

Agree/disagree: "A person does not do enough merely to acknowledge equality."

Agree/disagree: "All of the nation suffers when one person suffers the loss of civil rights."

Agree/disagree: "The people of culture are the true apostles of equality."—Matthew Arnold

Agree/disagree: "So far is it from being true that men are naturally equal, that no two people can be half an hour together, but one shall acquire an evident superiority over the other."

Argue whether any individual is indispensable.

Argue whether neighbors are necessary.

Argue for/against giving up one's religion for someone.

Discuss argumentatively the Biblical statement, "A prophet is not without honour, save in his own country, and in his own house."

Discuss argumentatively this quotation from Sir Thomas Browne: "Charity begins at home, is the voice of the world."

Agree/disagree: "Repudiate the repudiators."—William Pitt Fessenden

Argue for when it is best not to be frank.

Argue whether the world, as Wordsworth says, "is too much with us."

Argue the redeeming qualities of someone or something not considered as having any.

Argue what psychiatry has done for society.

Argue whether there is any use in society for Mother's Day and Father's Day.

Discuss argumentatively the quotation from Hart Crane: "For we can still love the world, who find a famished kitten on the step."

Argue for/against labor unions.

Argue for/against your joining a union.

Argue the worth of a certain city because of the things to do there.

Economy, Employment

Is anything ever yours "absolutely *free*"?

Discuss argumentatively the quotation from Professor Phumble: "Why pay-as-you-go when you don't go anywhere?"

Argue for/against a certain boycott.

Argue whether it is so that two can live as cheaply as one.

As a buyer for your company, try to persuade your boss to your opinion on a certain issue or plan.

Argue your worth to a certain employer.

Argue for/against merit promotion.

Argue for/against gold, or silver, as the money standard.

Argue whether there really is an energy crisis.

Argue what government spending should give priority to.

Argue for/against a national debt.

Argue what our assets are nationally.

Argue for/against subsidizing farms.

Argue for/against free bus travel for certain citizens over certain short routes.

Argue for/against subsidy for public transportation.

Argue for/against a certain tax reform.

Argue what the best place is for inexpensive living for the retired.

Argue for/against parking meters.

Argue for/against tipping.

Argue for/against the idea of *caveat emptor*.

Argue for/against farming as a profession.

Argue whether one should be exempted from high payments of car insurance if proven accident-free.

Argue who should, or who should not, keep receiving financial support from the government.

Discuss argumentatively this quotation from Thomas Jefferson: "Never spend your money before you have it."

Time and Eternity, Life Pursuits, Death and Life

Agree/disagree: "No man can serve two masters."—Bible.

Agree/disagree: "It is the best of all trades, to make songs, and the second best to sing them."—Hilaire Belloc

Argue for/against idlers and time-wasters.

Argue for a past custom that is worth bringing back.

Argue for/against the four-day work week.

Argue how one should spend time.

Argue for a particular pastime such as painting.

Agree/disagree: "If at first you don't succeed, quit and go fishing."

Argue what dreams there are to buy when dreams are for sale.

Agree/disagree: "One will endure who asks nothing of life."

Agree/disagree: "There is nothing wrong with chasing rainbows."

Discuss argumentatively the quotation from John Fletcher, "There is no drinking after death."

Agree/disagree: "In landlessness alone resides the highest truth."—Herman Melville

Argue how our lives would be different if there were no recorded history.

Argue whether modern people are significantly different from people of ancient times or of medieval times.

Argue for/against living for the moment.

Agree/disagree: Humanity will not only endure; it will prevail.—paraphrased from William Faulkner.

Agree/disagree: "Our life is frittered away by detail." —Thoreau

Agree/disagree: "It won't matter ten years from now."

Agree/disagree: "It's hell to be old in the United States."

Argue what age bracket takes success best.

Argue whether there is an age when a person can get by with just about anything.

Argue whether time is necessary for experience.

Argue whether fame is really fleeting.

Argue some contemporary question as if it were based in some prehistoric time—for example, the energy shortage during the period of the cave people.

Agree/disagree: "Your children are not your children. They are the sons and daughters of Life's longing for itself."—Khalil Gibran

Argue whether you should buy life insurance.

Agree/disagree: "The wise are always ready for death." (Jean De La Fontaine)

Agree/disagree: "Why fear death? It is the most beautiful adventure in life."—Charles Frohman

Agree/disagree on this attitude: "Death will come when it will come."

Argue whether life is a line, or a circle.

Argue what the milestones of life are.

Argue whether death is a milestone of life.

Argue for/against belief in life after life.

Agree/disagree: "It matters not how a man dies, but how he lives."—(Samuel Johnson)

Argue what you would do if you knew where and how you were going to die.

Argue for/against cremation rather than burial.

Argue the point technically and spiritually: When is death, when is life?

Discuss argumentatively this quotation from John Donne: "Death be not proud."

Discuss argumentatively this quotation from John Donne: "Death Thou shalt die."

Discuss argumentatively this quotation from the poet Omar Khayyam: "We know of death only when we travel its road."

Discuss argumentatively this quotation from the poet William Ernest Henley: "I am the master of my fate: I am the captain of my soul."

Discuss argumentatively this quotation from Samuel Johnson concerning ghosts: "All argument is against it; but all belief is for it."

Agree/disagree: "Nature's Time should be left as it is."

Agree/disagree: "Time is your best ally."

Argue whether you will always be the way you were created.

Discuss argumentatively this quotation from Vachel Lindsay: "To live in mankind is far more than to live in a name,
To live in mankind, far, far more than to live in a name."

Discuss argumentatively the argument that anthropologists make: that cultures do not stay the same but are in a continuous state of change.

Argue that time will show that _____.

Argue what in life, or in all eternity, is our greatest resource.

Discuss argumentatively this quotation from the "small society" cartoon: "If you can't handle a rainy weekend, how are you going to handle retirement?"

Discuss argumentatively this quotation from the "small society" cartoon: "If you don't learn to laugh at trouble . . . you won't have anything to laugh at when you grow old."

Discuss argumentatively this quotation from Robert Burns: "No one can tie time or tide."

Discuss argumentatively this attitude from the cartoon character Andy Capp: "By the time you've said Now, Now is Then," so go ahead, he suggests, and keep putting off things and go back to sleep.

DEFINITION

What Definition Is

Definition seeks to establish the limits or boundaries of a word as it is used in any given context. This book offers only the most immediate example of the topic at hand. Each introduction attempts to define a particular kind of writing for the specific purposes of this volume. Many approaches are used. Some may appear almost to throw off the dictionary meanings as they wrestle with the demands of circumstances, but each definition is etymologically rooted. The etymology of *definition* itself has to do with "bringing to an end." But no dictionary definition is definitive—not in a living language. It may determine the meaning(s) of a word for the time being, settle the boundaries of a word, but not its hash. Words are alive and they undergo the vicissitudes of any other living thing.

It might be helpful to think of definition as a way of describing a word (in terms of our approach to description, say, which appeared earlier in this book). Here again our ultimate aim is not to capture our subject—and certainly not to bring it to a permanent end—but to set it free. Definition is one of the spokes in the rhetorical wheel we have been spinning through these pages and (to give the analogy one final turn) it is also part of the hub grease that keeps the wheel turning freely.

How to Write Definition

Definition is not only a way of explaining a word clearly, precisely, concretely; it is also a way of exploring both the word and how it relates to its private context. Sometimes it seems we do not really know what a word means—or what it means to us—until we attempt to describe it on paper. Definition, much like any other form of writing, is a way of thinking and of discovering what we know. An essay in definition could hardly avoid, nonetheless, digging into the roots of a subject, investigating its history. That kind of groundwork tends to deepen a word, build its muscle, give it centuries of room in which to swing its arms.

Surely the writer ought always to know the meaning of any word he or she uses. In the age of what Orwell called "doublethink," definition is not only imperative but crucial. Can there ever be a *holy* war? Are people oppressed to be free? Are countries destroyed to be saved? By all means, let us define our terms.

Locating Subjects for Definition

Many of the subjects listed in this chapter are quotations. Often they are aphoristic and their sense depends upon word definitions that are at once stringent and free. Wrestling with some of them will be vigorous exercise, both for the muscle-bound writer and the writer whose loose-limbed prose sprawls all over the page.

Definition rightly claims its own spoke on that rhetorical wheel. But the crafty wheelwright will shape it clear round the rim. Argumentation, exposition, research and report, critical writing—none of these will get very far without some solid element of definition (though many will try). Nor does it stop there by any means: Anyone would want to write something that would as a whole become a definition of love, freedom, faith—or any of the other fires consuming the hearts of so many, lighting their souls.

Some Views of God for Definition

"An honest God is the noblest work of man."—Robert Ingersoll

"It is God's trade to pardon."—(paraphrased from Heinrich Heine)

"The Lord is a man of war."—Bible.

"The nature of God is a circle of which the center is everywhere and the circumference is nowhere." —Anonymous

God is.—(a common definition from Oriental thought)

God is the oldest of poets.—proverb

"The groves were God's first temples."—William Cullen Bryant

"Nature is the art of God."—Sir Thomas Browne

Human Beings and Human Types for Definition

A

Absent-minded professor, active person, agnostic, airline pilot, Fred Allen, Gracie Allen, amateur/professional, anonymous, army brat, atheist, athlete, auctioneer, average citizen

What are the criteria for judging a great actor?

How would you define the "earliest American"?

"We are all Armenians," said William Saroyan. What did he mean, in terms of definition?

A letter to an Albuquerque paper says that sportswriters who write about athletics at the University of New Mexico are "miserable, vindictive, whining losers and obnoxious winners." This "counterproductive" athletic program, the letter goes on to say, should be abolished. Discuss with reference to definition stereotypes about athletes and athletics.

B

Backwoods people, bad/good neighbor, top banana, Jack Benny, best friend (or dog's best friend), Big Brother as created by George Orwell, bookworm, Brand X, Eva Braun, George Burns

Discuss in terms of definition the fact that Mel Blanc created his voices from the beginning—before the cartoons.

What does it mean to define someone as a big person? Consider this cartoon item: "It takes a fat man to admit he's wrong," says Hagar's wife. No, no, insists Hagar, that expression is, "It takes a *big* man."

How would you define a Bostonian? Note Thomas Appleton's definition: "A Boston man is the east wind made flesh."

What stereotype definition is understood in this cartoon item?—"He doesn't know the meaning of the word fear, or anything else for that matter," a manager says of his boxer.

According to definition, is it possible for you to have a "jolly good time" if you are not British?

Discuss Jack Anderson's saying, "All the world's a stage and bureaucrats play it."

C

Cadillac, Cadjun, Calamity Jane, Canadians as seen by the Japanese, Lewis Carroll, Kit Carson, celebrity, Wilt Chamberlain, charlatan, Charlie Chaplin, Chief of Protocol, the child inside, Christ as seen by television and movies, Cleopatra, Joe College of the 50s, Crazy Jane as created by William Butler Yeats, Creole, Davy Crockett, Marie Curie

What does the following poetical definition tell you about the Cabots, the Lowells, and other Bostonians high and low?
"And this is good old Boston,
    The home of the bean and the cod.
Where the Lowells talk to the Cabots,
    And the Cabots talk only to God."
        John Collins Bossidy

Andy Capp the cartoon character doesn't just fall asleep in church, says his minister; he heckles. How would you define Andy Capp, or some other famous cartoon character?

"The Child is father of the Man," said William Wordsworth. What special definition of the child is Wordsworth using?

The Children's Crusade is a book about a real movement by 50,000 children in 1212 to stop war. How can this movement be defined in terms of what has happened in recent history?

The Chinese have stopped using the term *Mandarin* because it is too class-conscious. Define some class-conscious term formerly used in the United States.

Shirley Chisholm of the U.S. House of Representatives wants to be remembered, she says, for what she is able to do to help her constituents. What does her statement have to do with definition of the politician?

Explain the definition implied in the fact that certain churchgoers were reprimanded by the courts for making their "joyful noise unto the Lord" too loud.

A headline reads, Citizen Catches Police. Even if you do not know the subject of the article that follows, what fixed definitions come to your mind immediately?

Is the term "senior citizen" insulting?

A certain coach says that his team is number 2, not number 1. Another coach, referring to his playing a team now that formerly trounced his team, says that revenge does not fit into his vocabulary. Discuss both these coaches in terms of definition.

Can we take the following quotation from Ebenezer Elliott as a contemporary definition of a communist? "What is a communist? One who has yearnings for equal divisions of unequal earnings."

George Eliot said that conceited people carry their comfort around with them. How would you define a conceited person?

What do conservatives usually denounce about society?

What does it say about modern definition that a man legally had his name changed from Cooperman to Cooperperson?

Is there any difference between a moral coward and a physical coward? Can a coward be brave and moral? Define in your own terms what a coward is. First of all, however, see what two reviews have said about the subject: *Newsweek* magazine says that the book *Catch-22* is about a "brave coward of high principle." A *TV Guide* review of the Black musical *Cindy* says: "The black-market chauffeur admits to Cindy's charge that he is a coward, noting that if the Japanese had been cowards there would be no war and adding: 'Cowards don't hurt people, don't start trouble, don't commit crimes. Cowards don't even double park.' "

Of Norm Crosby, the modern Mr. Malaprop, Cleveland Amory writes: "It's not doubletalk," Crosby declared, "it's word substitution. All I do is take the proper word and use it in an improper way—like 'women need tenderness and affliction,' or 'singers project from their diagram.' " Define Norm Crosby so as to explain why he is known as Mr. Malaprop.

A typographical error in a newspaper changed Dr. Cunningham to Dr. Cunning. How do accidents about our names sometimes wrongly define us?

Tony Curtis says that he never said in a movie, "Yonda lies da castle o' my fodda." What popular image of his is he quarreling with?

D

Democrat/Republican, dilettante, do-gooder, dreamer, drone, dunce

Define what a doctor is in light of the following: Is a PhD, a Doctor of Philosophy, a doctor? "Over-Doctor" is the Japanese term for an overeducated, unplaced, unemployable PhD.

A certain doctor is asked if she makes condominium calls. What modern definition is forced on the usual definition of doctor?

"Every physician almost hath his favourite disease," Henry Fielding wrote in the eighteenth century. Does his statement still define the doctor, in part?

"Anger makes dull men witty," said the first Queen Elizabeth. How do you define a dull person?

E

Each and everyone, early riser, easy rider, eccentric, emigrant-immigrant, worst enemy, everyone a stranger

A certain entertainer's talent is that he can make himself look like any make of car. What other entertainer do you know who is defined by an unusual talent?

Everyone has some kind of handicap, it has been said. In what important ways can everyone be defined as being like everyone else?

F

Face in the crowd, Fascist under Mussolini (contrasted with Fascist as used loosely during the 60s), fair weather friend, Our Father Who (Our Father, Who?), faun, Fenian, Millard Fillmore, Flim Flammer, flower child, football widow

What face is on a certain coin or bill? Why *that* face on that item rather than another face?

What can one do to determine human definition when the following is true?—"It is the common wonder of all men, how among so many millions of faces, there should be none alike."—Sir Thomas Browne

What is there in the definition of television evangelism that allows us to accept that faith-healers leave huge estates when they die?

"The family that prays together stays together." Discuss this slogan, or another that it reminds you of, so as to indicate that slogans do not define particularly but only generally. (One example of this fact: The Manson group called itself a family and had its own kind of prayers.)

How do movies about the famous portray them?

To what extent has the attitude expressed in the following statement (by H.L. Mencken, the famous journalist) become a stereotyped definition of the farmer?—"The only political idea he can grasp is one which promises him a direct profit."

What is there in recent history that links, in definition, the American farmers with the hippies of the 1960s?

If you are on file somewhere, are you therefore defined as no more than the file says you are? Are you merely the sum of the personal items mentioned there?

W.C. Fields was democratic: he hated everyone equally. What playful, complete definition do we have of W.C. Fields on the basis of his movies and popular image?

The Bible says "A fool utters all his mind" and "Answer a fool according to his folly." What, by your definition, is a fool?

How do descriptions of us sometimes limit or confound what we are? Note that sometimes people get swallowed up by name and town descriptions of them: "With him is his wife the former Mary Smith of Johnsonville." Does the word *former* mean that Mary no longer exists? Is Johnsonville where she lives *now* or where she used to live?

F

Vancouver Gets Fortier, a headline announces, with reference to Dave Fortier, hockey professional. Is getting Fortier anything like getting Twentier? How can our names comically define us?

What, in definition, is behind the fact that Franklin is the name most used in naming American towns?

G

Geek, Georgia Cracker, gift horse, God as defined by a child, a pastor named God, a great person, Lady Jane Grey (The Nine Days' Queen), Che Guevara, guru, Gutenberg

How would you define a genius? Does a genius have time for the ordinary world? Is everyone a genius? Does genius require only a high IQ? Is a genius very much different from you and me? "To know what a genius is," says a GE advertisement, "ask a genius." "Genius is of no country," said Charles Churchill.

Define a gospel singer as someone who does more than make "a joyful noise unto the Lord."

Define a grave (serious) person after consulting this quotation from G.K. Chesterton: "It is really a natural trend to lapse into taking oneself gravely, because it is the easiest thing to do; for solemnity flows out of men naturally, but laughter is a leap. It is easy to be heavy; hard to be light. Satan fell by force of gravity."

What defines a great person? Is it misleading to call persons the "all-time greatest" in their fields? What definition enters into the idea in this quotation from Robinson Jeffers?—"Greatness is but less little; and death's changed life."

H

Ham actor, radio ham, harlequin, Hatfields and McCoys, Henry the Eighth's wives, Hitler as seen by a teenager, homebody, howitzer

Some people float on salt water; others, such as Hagar the cartoon character, bounce. Add many details about Hagar to help define him in the minds of others.

Give a deliberately stereotyped definition of a hero. To understand the stereotype is to understand, as well, what is not a stereotype.

Is the idea of the dying hero romantic or realistic?

A "hooker" in a steel plant hooks crates for hoisting. Ignoring the contemporary definition of "hooker," discuss, in definition terms, what has happened to another term accidentally associated with at least two different types.

After considering the following quotation from Ferdinand Foch, define the term *human soul*: "The most powerful weapon on earth is the human soul on fire."

Using definition, argue whether hypocrites know that they are hypocrites.

I

Indiana Hoosier, indispensable person, intellectual, Irish, Ivy Leaguer of the 1950s

Indians Hoard Artifacts, says a headline. What does the headline do to reverse the stereotype about Indians? Take some cliché or stereotype about the Indian and, by definition, refute it.

Define by comparison/contrast an Indian from India and an Indian from the United States or Canada.

What is an innocent? Is it the same in definition as an innocent person? How do we behave towards people who have been tried as criminals but have been found innocent?

J

Jingoist, "Job's Comforter," Elton John, "just plain folks," Supreme Court Justice, Jute, juvenile

Jesse James was formerly the Treasurer of Texas, and he was replaced by someone who also had a famous name, Warren G. Harding. How might definition affect someone who has the same name made famous by someone else?

Define Justice _____, United States Supreme Court.

K

Franz Kafka, Walt Kelly, Kilroy, Olga Korbut

Distinguish, by definition, between the Kafir people of Africa and the Kafir people of Afghanistan.

Define *kaiser* by way of its etymology.

Define the kamikaze pilot in religious and patriotic terms, not just historically.

Define the Katzenjammer Kids of comic-strip fame.

Define *khedive* in general, but strictly historical, terms.

What is a kibitzer?

What, in *modern* terms, is a knave?

How does Kriss Kringle differ, in definition, from Santa Claus?

How are the Kurdish people related to the Iranian people?

L

Doris Lessing, look-alike, The Lost Generation, Low Churchman, Low German, Lucifer, Luke of the Bible, Martin Luther of the Reformation

"Lawyers talk, but it is their business to talk," said Thomas Jefferson. James Boswell said of the lawyer that he "has no business with the justice or injustice of the cause which he undertakes, unless his client ask his opinion, and then he is bound to give it honestly. The justice or injustice of the cause is to be decided by the judge." How do these statements define what a lawyer is in ways opposed to a stereotyped definition? How do you define a lawyer?

Left-handed Ken Stabler has beaten insurmountable odds, says Jim Murray the sportswriter. He is a successful professional quarterback in spite of being a lefty—and in spite of having been born on Christmas. Is there any way to define left-handed people generally?

What does a liberal denounce about society? How does this denunciation define what a liberal is? How is an English liberal opposed to an American liberal?

Why is Guy Lombardo defined in the minds of many people so that he is connected with the New Year?

Does the Lone Ranger grow old as a part of his definition?

Define *Lord Chancellor.*

Define *lord of misrule.*

What would be a good example of a modern lotus-eater?

What would be a good example of a modern "Lot's Wife"?

Define *lowbrow.*

What would be a good example of a modern Lynceus?

M

Machiavelli, The Real McCoy, mask (meaning *persona*), Somerset Maugham, a human maverick, Ken Maynard, someone without a middle name, minister's child, Minnesota Fats, Martha Mitchell, a mod person, Thomas More as seen by his contemporary opposition, someone voted "Most Happy in High School Class," someone voted Most Likely to Succeed, mutual friend(s), someone morally myopic

What misdefinitions can you find in the following quotation from Texas Governor Ma Perkins?—"English was good enough for the Bible; it ought to be good enough for the Meskins too."

Discuss the definition of *man* as implied by the following: "In lapidary inscriptions a man is not upon oath." —Samuel Johnson

An instructor at Yale figures he is the real "$6 million man," considering the prices of the various chemical components of his body according to his height, weight, and so forth.

Clothes make (or do not make) the man, woman, person.

A certain man wants to be known as 1069, a newspaper item reports.

A newspaper item tells of a man who agreed to become another person to please passport officials who kept giving him a name other than his own.

"My favourite, I might say, my only study, is man." —George Borrow

Benjamin Franklin said of humanity that there are "those who are immovable; those who are movable; those who move."

Define who Mao's widow is, taking into account that she is known more as "Mao's widow" rather than by her name.

Define *media person.* Who are, or what are, the media?

Do men or women who are great know they are great? Define *great men, great women.*

Give your own definition of *metaphysician* after noting the following: A metaphysician, said Charles, Baron Bowen, is "a blind man in a dark room—looking for a black hat—which isn't there."

Who are the mild?

Did early monks speak in script?

The actor Ricardo Montalban insists on keeping his Latin accent so as to keep his dignity. How were earlier actors defined by their accents or their origins so that they became stereotyped?

Who is the "mother of all living"?

You probably don't know the last names of the cartoon characters Mutt and Jeff. What does that fact tell you about their definition?

What is meant, in terms of definition, by someone's saying, "I'm not myself today"? Is there only one *myself* for each person? What are the differences in definition among the pronouns *me, myself,* and *I* as they refer to a single person? Is there any difference between *my self* and *myself*?

Give an elaborate definition of *mystagogue.*

Define someone who is said to be "a mystery."

Write an extended definition of a modern mystic.

Write about a mythical person as if he or she were defined by the real world.

Define *mythomaniac.*

N

A human nag, a single Nahuatl, a naiad as a real person, a *naïf,* someone who is a namesake, a modern (and real) Narcissus, Carry Nation, native, a "natural" for one pursuit or another, a literary naturalist, a single Navaho, Nazi, Neanderthal man, Queen Nefertiti, neighbor, neophyte, a modern (and real) Nestor, a neurotic, a "new face" or a "new kid on the block," a 19th-century nihilist, a nit-picker, nitwit, a noble, the Noble Savage as defined by the eighteenth and nineteenth centuries, a nobody, Nobody (in a "Vote for Nobody" drive), a nonagenarian, a nondescript, a nonesuch, the "Royal Nonesuch" of Mark Twain's *Huckleberry Finn,* a Norman, *nouveau riche,* someone who is just a number

After considering the following, discuss definition according to names and nicknames:

A newspaper item says that a man has 10-8 as his first name.

Will the real _____ stand up?

Are persons who change their names different persons?

How long does it take for a changed name to catch on?

Secret names are often used for protecting highly placed officials and those close to them.

Sometimes, two or more persons with the same names run for the same public office.

In Sweden, 40 percent of the population shares twenty names all of which end in *-son.*

What would you expect of someone named for, say, Watergate?

Who is No-Man? Who is Everyman? Who is Everywoman?

When names of certain streets named for certain persons are misspelled, what happens to definition?

There were hundreds of ways in Shakespeare's time

to spell his name. Would Shakspeer by any other name still be as great a writer?

Don Coryell May Become a Saint, says a headline, referring to the coach's possibly joining the New Orleans Saints, a professional football team. Take into account how some names invite puns: Beane, Soldier, Tree, and so forth.

What is behind a certain nickname?

What's *not* in a name? What's in a name?

Is it possible for someone to have the wrong name?

Define the New Yorker in a deliberately stereotyped way; then define a specific New Yorker.

Define *nonresident* better than the following definition (from a New York City document) does: "A non-resident individual means an individual who is not a resident."

O

Oberon, Oceanus, a modern (and real) Odysseus, an Ojibway Indian, Oklahoma Sooner, only child, oneself (by an extended version of the second dictionary definition), Orangeman, a modern (and real) Orpheus, outlaw, Oxonian, Ozymandias

In a cartoon, the old woman in a shoe gives an account of what her children, now grown, are doing. Define in your own terms what the "old woman who lived in a shoe" is like.

"You optimists are all alike," says a cartoon figure to a sign carrier whose sign reads: Doomsday Is Near. Define *optimist*.

Define *ordinary people*.

Define a particular Oriental.

Define someone thought of as an "original."

P

Pacifist, pagan, a modern and real Pan, a modern and real Pandora, a modern and real Pantagruel, paragon, Parnassian of the second half of the 19th century, partisan, pastor, patriot, patron saint, a modern and real Pecksniff, a peripatetic, the person inside, person of trust, person on the street, a whole person, *persona*, pessimist, philistine (in the modern sense), Pict, a carnival pitchman, an individual Polynesian, pooh-bah, prima donna, prince, a modern and real Prometheus, Prufrock, psychotic, Puritan

What are the criteria for defining a great painter?

What are the criteria for defining a great philanthropist?

What are the criteria for defining a great philosopher?

Can a philosopher be a philosopher without preaching philosophy?

What are the criteria for defining a great poet?

Define *poet* as William Cullen Bryant does in saying "Every individual is more or less a poet."

Can a poet be a poet without writing poetry?

Who are the poor? Are there legal terms that, in the United States, define who the poor are and who the

wealthy are? What does it mean that the poor, by definition, have to have money just to be poor?

President Ford could have named Vice-President Nelson Rockefeller as President in his last days in office. Are there other ways in which a President might be said to hold an ambiguous office?

What person is the most glorified professional person in the United States?

"A rottenness begins in the conduct of a man who casts his eye longingly on public office," said Thomas Jefferson. How do you define *public servant*?

Q

Quacksalver, Quaker, Quixote

R

Rabelais, ragamuffin, Raphael, a literary realist, revivalist, a modern and real Rip Van Winkle, Norman Rockwell, the Rosenbergs, an individual Russian

Define any robber baron, especially in terms of American history.

Define *role-player*. Is everyone a role-player in some way?

S

Sacred cow, sad sack, sage, saint, Samaritan, a modern and real sandman, the Biblical Sarah, Satan, scapegoat, scoundrel, Seabee, second but not least, Section Eight (as defined to 1944 in the United States Army), self-image, self-made person, sepoy, skipper, slyboots, smart aleck, John Smith (of whom there are more than 60,000 in the United States), Joseph Smith's wives, spieler, a stage version of anyone (such as a hero, a villain, an Irishman, a drunkard), Stagedoor Johnny, Stradivarius, Billy Sunday, Superman, suzerain, swashbuckler

How might a child seeing a different Santa at every street corner define Santa Claus?

"She is the youngest of four brothers," says a newspaper item. Define the *she* of this quotation.

Which person is defined as the football player, O.J. Simpson or Orenthal James Simpson?

"For she was the maker of the song she sang," wrote Wallace Stevens. How do you define *singer*? What makes a great singer?

Define *social climber*.

Define *sponge* in human terms.

Can a sport be a sport without participating in sports?

"I refuse to be bent, folded, spindled, or mutilated," said a student, who was concerned about having to fill out so much computer information. How might a computer define a student?

Define *style-setter*.

T

An individual Tagalog, tallyman, a modern and real Tarzan, a television critic, a tenement dweller, Texas

Ranger, a thief who steals Bibles, a modern and real Thor, tourist, trickster (as from fables and folklore), troubadour, troubleshooter, tycoon, type, tyrant

What definition was a little girl making when she asked her teacher what she had dressed up as for Hallowe'en?

Is it true that the teacher who is defined as the "meanest" and most demanding of the students is the one who is the most respected?

"There is no 'them,' just lots of 'us,'" said Swami Baba Rum-Dum. How are *them*, *they*, and *us* defined?

Define a modern-day Thwackum, a glimpse of whom is seen in this quotation from Henry Fielding: "Thwackum was for doing justice, and leaving mercy to heaven."

A newspaper item says that the Transylvanians accept werewolves and vampires as fact. Define *Transylvanian* as if you were an expert about, or an enthusiast for, horror tales.

Define *twin* so as to make a clear distinction between the twin you define and the twin who is that twin's twin.

U

Ugly duckling, a modern and real Ulysses as a compulsive wanderer, Unknown Citizen, Unknown Soldier, a utilitarian

A man who won an "Ugliest Man" contest says that he "looks forward to becoming still uglier." Discuss his statement in terms of definition.

Who is one of the "undecided" even *after* an election is over?

V

Vagabond, Valkyrie, vassal, vaudevillian, veep, Vice-President Who, viceroy, victim, Viking, villain, vulgarian

Define Gore Vidal, taking into consideration the title of an article about him, "With Malice Towards Some and Charity for Few."

Certain army recruiting officers have admitted to inventing phony volunteers in order to meet their quota obligations. How might such a volunteer (non-existent, remember) who got onto the army rolls be defined?

W

WAF, waif, Mike Wallace "the jugular journalist," Walloon, Wandering Jew, WAVE, Weird Sisters, Whig, whipping boy, Walt Whitman as Everyone, whiz, wizard, wunderkind

XYZ

Xanthippe, Yahoo, Yankee as seen by a Latin American, yes-man, yeti, yogi, you as seen by your best friend and then as seen by your enemy, *your self* as distinguished from *yourself*, youth, zombie, Zouave

Human Conditions, Human Relations, Sociology

aging, alcoholism, Apocalypse, backlash, bandwagon, the big sleep, blackout (as used during World War II), blessing in disguise, bundling, catbird seat, challenge, Christmas as a symbol of the American culture, circumspection, class, code-living, commencement ceremony (as a beginning), competition, conflict, consistency, contemplation, conventionalism, coordination, cost of war, cult, culture shock, death, dog days, ecotactics, enrichment, environment, escapism, ethnic purity, etiquette (as opposed to "manners"), fad, failure (as defined by an American), feedback, Fifth Column, *fin de siecle* mood, fixed idea, flag-waving, The Four Horsemen, generation gap, gluttony, gossip, grass roots, gullibility, hassle, heart, heartland, heredity, hiatus, hoarding (as in wartime), hoopla, human, human being, human condition, humanity, hypocrisy, idea, illumination, implication, incomplete investigation, inference, informality, innocence (as opposed to sophistication), introspection, involvement, jamboree, jealousy, jeopardy, judgment (*not* justice), justice, kindness, knowledge, kosher, life (including life after death and life after life), light as knowledge, light pollution, love, *machismo*, marriage-go-round, marriage of convenience, marriage to one's (job, motorcycle, pastime), meditation, meeting one's Waterloo, mellowness, Mexican *mordida*, middle-of-the-road, moderation as excess, moral cowardice, moratorium, negligence, neutrality, new morality, new wave, noise pollution, notoriety/ infamy, obedience, oblivion, old money/new money, over a barrel, pain, panhandling, panic, parasitism, paternalism, pedantry, permissiveness, prejudice, primogeniture, privacy, private Utopia, puberty, pushiness, quintessence, raisin in the sun, ready for love/in love with love, recession, reclamation, relevance, responsibility, rumor, sacrifice, scandal, "semi-happiness," sense of place, sensibility, sentiment, sentimentality, September song, serendipity, showdown, sluggishness, success (as defined by an American), swan song, taboo, tact, carrying the torch/passing the torch, troubleshooting, the ultimate adventure, uncouthness, utilitarianism, vindication, wit/humor/sense of humor, wonder/awe/amazement, Zeno's nine paradoxes, zero population growth

Draw subjects for definition from the following items about the human condition:

Augustine said that total abstinence is easier than perfect moderation.

"Anger is a short madness."—Horace

Define "Black humor"—not in the usual way but with reference to the humor of Blacks.

How does Emerson's phrase "the blowing clover, the falling rain" relate to the human condition?

"Boldness is a child of ignorance and baseness." —Sir Francis Bacon

"Boldness is an ill keeper of promise."—Sir Francis Bacon

"Being busy is a national excuse as well as a national passion."—Norman Cousins

Is there anyone or anything in the human condition that cannot be captured—that is, defined and understood—in a book?

What is a "worthy cause" in these days when almost everything is said to be one?

"Character is destiny."—Novalis

Define the "chasing-after-the-dream" syndrome.

"Give me chastity and continency," said St. Augustine, "but do not give it yet."

Common sense, someone has said, is uncommon sense.

"No true compassion without will, no true wit without compassion."—John Fowles

"Conscience is a coward, and those faults it has not strength enough to prevent it seldom has justice enough to accuse."—Oliver Goldsmith

What makes cool? You are cool if you _____.

"Courageous the pine that does not change its color under winter snow."—Hirohito (*Time*, October 4, 1971)

"Death, in itself, is nothing; but we fear,/To be we know not what, we know not where."—Dryden

"Deeds, not words, shall speak me."—John Fletcher

"You have delighted us long enough," says Mr. Bennet to his daughter, who is entertaining the company in the novel by Jane Austen, *Pride and Prejudice*.

What in your opinion is the "whole duty" of a person?

"Rightly understood, freedom is the universal license to be good."—(paraphrased from lines by Hartley Coleridge)

"Freedom is unbelievably precious."—(the Soviet seaman, now free in the United States, who once was captured by the Soviets when he tried to escape from them)

Define *future shock* as it relates to the human condition.

"What is the worth of anything,/But for the happiness 'twill bring?"—Richard Cambridge

"Heredity," says a newspaper item, "is what you believe in when your child gets A's in school."

Define *Honi soit qui mal y pense* as the statement relates to the human condition.

What is "honourable" as it is used in the title of John le Carré's novel *The Honourable Schoolboy*?

"Humanity is immense, and reality has a myriad of forms."—Henry James

How has the term "innocence" come to have negative connotations?

Can intelligence be defined as proportion?

"Justice was invented by criminals."—Dashiell Hammett

"To live in hearts we leave behind is not to die."—Thomas Campbell

"Love speaks in smiles," says the Charmers newspaper panel.

"Love's tongue is in the eyes."—Phineas Fletcher

"I loved not yet, yet I loved to love. . . . I sought what I might love, in love with loving."—St Augustine

How accurate is the definition of love in I Corinthians 13?

"Ever has it been that love is master where he will."—John Gower

Are diamonds really "forever," as in the advertisements? What about those that are "broken" by the dissolution of a love match?

Define what is meant by Shakespeare's saying that one should "choose love by another's eye."

An idea from Daniel Defoe is to love the subject for the sake of the teacher. Illustrate and define love put in a similar context.

"There is no crime as shameful as poverty."—(paraphrase of a line in George Farquhar)

"Prosperity is not without many fears and distastes; and adversity is not without comforts and hopes."—Sir Francis Bacon

"Reputation is an idle and most false imposition, oft got without merit and lost without deserving."—Shakespeare

Referring to sleep, Sir Thomas Browne said: "The brother of death exacts a third part of our lives."

"The strongest reason best."—Jean De La Fontaine

"A tart temper never mellows with age, and a sharp tongue is the only edged tool that grows keener with constant use."—Washington Irving

"Treason doth never prosper: What's the reason? For if it prosper, none dare call it treason."—Sir John Harington

"The tree will wither long before it fall."—Lord Byron

Non-Human Life/Creatures

aardvark, aardwolf, adder, Afghan hound, albatross, alpaca, amoeba, anaconda, ant bear, antelope, ape, armadillo, auk, baboon, bacterium, bee eater, beetle, bighorn, bison, blenny, buffalo, cat, chicken snake, cicada, clam, conch, crab, cygnet, dinosaur, dog-faced butterfly, a cross between a donkey jenny and a zebra stallion, dove, dragonfly, drake, duck, elephant, fox, gander, heron, ibex, the mythical jabberwock, kite, kiwi, lizard, lobster, mealybug, mink, myna or mynah, nanny goat, okapi, prairie dog, puffin, quail, razorbill, sea horse, springer spaniel, squab, staghound, tick, Galapagos turtle, the mythical unicorn, vulture, warthog, weevil, right whale, yellow jacket, zebra fish

Draw subjects for definition from the following items about creature life:

"Bull fighting is not a sport. It is a tragedy."—Ernest Hemingway

Two headlines: Bulldogs Battle Demons Today *and* Scorpions Trounce the Eagles

Are cats wrongly maligned?

Do chimpanzees really talk, or do they merely imitate their human teachers?

Dagwood learns of a fish called the goby: the older it gets the smaller it gets: and when it disappears, it's full-grown.

Look over the first paragraph of Dickens' *Hard Times* for the stereotyped definition and the natural definition of a horse. Then write a stereotyped definition of any non-human creature, followed by an opposing, and natural, definition.

How did the peacock gets its reputation?

Does a pet know its name?

Does a racehorse know it is a racehorse?

When is an animal "rare"?

Psychology and the Mind, Emotions

abnormality, after-vacation blues, astro-soul, blood lust, blue Monday, brain waves, child's nightmares, conscience, ego, "emotional cannibalism" (from Henry James), exploitation, fanaticism, *gestalt*, guilty conscience, hijacker, syndrome, hostage syndrome, id, insanity, instability, instinct, intelligence quotient, intuition, love/hate relationship, mania, manipulation, narcissism, neuroticism, normality, personality, perversion, psychiatry, psychology, psychotherapy, sanity, Skinner's "behaviorism," social friction, sour grapes, spring fever, superego, triskaidekaphobia, *Zeitgeist*

Ambiguity, Ambivalence, Infinity, Measurelessness, Ubiquity

Write an extended definition of one of these terms: about/nearly/hardly, ambiguity, ambivalence, anachronism, drop in the ocean, energy, euphemism, exoticism, fat/plump, hard side/soft side, hypothesis, imagination, impossibility, infinity, insight, -ism, kaleidoscope, less/few, malapropism, measurelessness, metaphysics, mirage sale, mogjup, mutually exclusive, nomadic syntax (used by the journalist Tom Wicker to refer to Eisenhower's rambling public pronouncements), phenomenon, Pyrrhic victory, rare/unusual, reality, reasonable/unreasonable, semi-terrific, something that stays, sprezzatura, symbol, thief of time, tomorrow/yesterday, ubiquity, unknown quality, unknown quantity, up/down, wacky names, want-ad terms, weather

Draw subjects for definition from the following items:

Write a comparison/contrast definition between an old airplane and a modern kite, in which the kite comes out the better of the two.

Discuss the ambiguities in these defining parts: "used car" in "used car salesman"; "easy" in "easy chair"; "small animal" in "small animal hospital"; "match" in "match box"; "hot" in "hot cup of coffee"; "good" in "good and angry."

Write of a characteristic problem arising from imprecise or ambiguous language in documents.

Are the terms *degree* and *ordination* ambiguous? Consider that Kirby J. Hensley has a mail-order business of ordaining people in the Universal Life Church. A newspaper article says of him: "He says he has ordained 6.5 million people and provided them with ministerial credentials for free-will offerings or fees for various advanced titles since his operation began in 1962."

Illustrate the ambiguity in each of the following; then write a definition essay discussing ways to eliminate ambiguity where it is not intended:

There wasn't a single man present.

She sold Mark Twain books.

A headline reads, Begin Conceding While Sadat Waits.

A government questionnaire says: "If your answer to the above question is yes, explain why not."

What is the most coveted award?

"Play ball!" says the king in *Wizard of Id*—to ball-and-chainers who are poised to beat one another.

Why are Darwin's definitions of beauty and love circular and therefore incomplete?

"Beauty is momentary in the mind—/The fitful tracing of a portal;/But in the flesh it is immortal." —Wallace Stevens

"Beauty is in the eye of the beholder."—Margaret Hungerford

"A thing of beauty is a joy forever."—John Keats

Are the stars beautiful up close?

"Beauty is its own excuse for being."—Ralph Waldo Emerson

"Beauty passes like a dream."—William Butler Yeats

"Beauty stands in the admiration only of weak minds led captive."—John Milton

When is big small? When is small big?

According to Montaigne, the thumb is the most important finger. Can the head commit a revolution from the body? Define the most important part of the body.

Show that "both sides" are not necessarily all sides.

Is Bugs Bunny as indigenous to American culture as Will Rogers is?

Note the definitions of these words, which either sound or look nearly alike: *ceras, cereous, ceres, Cereus, cerous, cerris, ceruse, cirrous, cirrus, scirrhous, scirrhus, Sciurus, series, serious, serous, siris.*

"When it is not necessary to change," said Viscount Falkland, "it is necessary not to change."

"What is character but the determination of incident? What is incident but the illustration of character?" —Henry James

Discuss the change of definition of the word *chauvinism* since its origin.

What does it really and specifically mean to think as a child?

What logic do children use in choices of words—such as "snew" as the past tense of the verb "snow"?

How do children know when they are children? Does a "child" have to be a child?

What is the popular image definition of Christ? Mohammad? Buddha?

When is clockwise counter-clockwise?

Choosing paint (especially its colors) gets tougher all the time because of the great number of different shades and the names for them. Define some colors other than the primary ones.

An absent comma makes all the difference in this sentence from a newspaper account of a political barbecue: "It should be an interesting day to say the least." Define a punctuation mark by considering its importance.

Can a computer end someone's life? How, in such a case, can it be defined?

A new definition of the word *copies* is *duplicate originals*, as Xerox refers to them.

Define the point-of-view involved in definition. Consider, for example, among many possibilities for illustration, that everyone is a number of persons all in one. A mother is also, or can be, a grandmother, an aunt, a sister, a wife, a daughter, and so forth. Of course she has an infinity of definition in addition to these: She may be a speed-reader, a horse enthusiast, a beauty, an Egyptologist, a Democrat, and so forth *ad infinitum*.

What is the opposing definition of the view that the Grand Canyon is merely a "heck of a hole in the ground"?

Take certain terms and give them new definitions. Can you make these definitions seem to fit?

Does the number of words define the value of a document? There are 1322 words in the Declaration of Independence, and there are 26,911 words in a certain government document regulating the sale of cabbages.

Define something that has at least two opposing names. "Stardust," for example, is also called "atmospheric contaminants."

What is the result of reversing the principal parts of a proverb? (Example: What goes down must come up.)

Ask the question, "What does *that* mean?" to some important something that needs definition. Then write the definition that answers your question.

The power to define is the power to cure, says William Raspberry, syndicated columnist. He gives as examples: "school districts that cure the problem of non-learning not by improved teaching but by setting lower standards; social statisticians who cure poverty not by improving income but by reassessing the assets of those who are impoverished. . . . The prospects are endless. Robbers could be transmuted into income-transfer specialists. Joblessness could be redefined as full-time leisure. Racial animosity could be ethno-tension. . . ."

When she married again, Elizabeth Taylor sold the diamond Richard Burton had given her. This is an illustration of the fact that things have definitions of different kinds at different times and under different circumstances.

Explain the confused definition in the following: A character in the comic strip *Pogo* says, "Financially we's in arrears," to which another character responds, "Didn't think we had a leg to stand on."

Distinguish, by definition, between the terms "lower depths" and "the pits."

Franklin discovered, not invented, electricity. Write comparison/contrast definitions of *discovery* and *invention*.

An old hymn by Jane Taylor says that it is "quite a disgrace to be fine." How could it possibly be a disgrace to be fine?

How would you define distance in the context of outer space?

How might *divorce* be defined, as used in the headline, Man Divorced from Army?

"Do one to others as you would have them do one to you," said an elementary student.

Define *doctor's excuse* when it refers to the excuse the doctor has for an absence of the doctor.

What could be defined as a case of "double reverse discrimination"?

How big, by definition, is a drop? How many half-drops make a drop?

Which way is east? west? north? south?

What defines empty? Are there empty spaces?

Enchiladas are the turkey of Mexico's Christmas dinner.

"Our friend, the enemy."—Beranger

How would you define *fad*? How do fads define us?

Is it possible to be mildly fanatical?

The outstanding farmer of the year, according to a cartoon, is the one who had the lowest loss.

"We are now going to hear the Chopin waltz in a flat," said a radio announcer. How did his improper emphasis lead to a misdefinition?

Define something by using the word *fradnip* to name it. (A *fradnip* is a term used as a substitute for any other term.)

Plato in the comic strip *Beetle Bailey* is asked to paint *friendship* on the side of a van, but he gets carried away and writes instead a treatise over the entire vehicle: "Friendship is a bridge . . . "

"The future becomes the present, the present the past, and the past turns into everlasting regret if you don't plan for it."—(Tennessee Williams, in *The Glass Menagerie*)

An occupational dictionary has dropped references to gender in a recent edition. How is this a consequence of modern definition?

What were the "good old times"? Were they as good as people say they were?

A newspaper asks whether government is the incompetent's best friend.

When everything is grotesque is nothing grotesque?

"The hand that signed the paper felled a city," said Dylan Thomas. How do you define *hand* as it is used in this statement?

What is the "height of the ridiculous"? About eighty feet?

In 1682, Virginia said that slavery was "hereditary."

How high are the stars in the world inside each of us?

"History is a nightmare from which I am trying to awaken."—James Joyce

Your home is your castle. Is a king's castle his home?

Is "How much can I get for it?" a definition of "sentimental value"?

Give definitions of "How are you?" and "How do you do?"

"Impression is nine-tenths of the law," says David Rife. What definitions are changed by this pun?

What is "in" this year? What is "out" or "not in" this year?

An Irish bar in Seattle is run by Japanese; the original owner died fifty years ago.

Define an intangible something by using concrete terms or by giving it a concrete aspect.

Define an intangible of a concrete something.

"A joke's a very serious thing."—Charles Churchill.

"That kitten smells black," said Diane Ephthimiou. Are some things identifiable by similar ambivalence of the senses?

Show by definition how contradictory and confusing the English language is. Some examples: *man's laughter* and *manslaughter* (pointed out by Mario Pei the linguist) and "It took a *month* of *fast talk* to convince them."

Young Twins Develop Own Language, says a newspaper item. How might such a language achieve a private definition?

Chamber of Commerce language changes into hippie slogans, and vice-versa, said Bronowski.

When, by definition, might a person be said to know two languages equally well, that is, be bilingual?

When is less more? When is more less?

"Life has a lot more meaning since taking the Dale Carnegie course," says an advertisement. Did "Life," as the quotation says, take the course? How is definition often confused by misplaced modifiers?

Where does the light go when the switch is turned off?

If you lose a key, is the key itself lost? What defines being "lost"?

Intangible though it is, love can be measured and therefore defined. How?

What is a "low dudgeon"—as opposed to a high dudgeon?

The golfer Gary Player's definition of luck is: "The more you practice, the luckier you get."

Thursday, July 7, 1977, was a day that came up all sevens—7-7-77—and was thus a lucky day, even for those who were, say, celebrating their thirteenth wedding anniversary.

"The map is not the territory it symbolizes."—Hayakawa

The mind does not act separately from the body like a "ghost in the machine," said Gilbert Ryle.

There is only one witness to what goes on in the mind in thought or dream.

"It [the mind] has memory's ear that can hear without having to hear."—(Marianne Moore, "The Mind Is an Enchanted Thing")

"In the old days," says a newspaper item, "if you saved money you were a miser; now you're a marvel."

February is the worst month of all, it is said, because it brings depression, boredom, and flu. What kind of month is April? What are April showers to different people of different ages? What is behind the quotation from T.S. Eliot's long poem "The Waste Land": "April is the cruellest month"? Write an extended definition for one of the months of the year.

Is the greatness of a museum dependent on the number of bricks it has?

What are some "new words for old deceptions"?

Discuss the difference in definition between "Newfoundland" and "New Found Land."

"That noise scared my ears," said Alden Powell. What definition does this quotation give to the sense of hearing?

Define literally such non-literal expressions as "Keep on your toes."

Write a definition essay showing that nothing is like anything else; that anything is unlike anything else.

Write a definition essay on *number(s)* after reading the following: "Round numbers are always false," said Samuel Johnson. "The half is greater than the whole," said Hesiod. A famous performer of mental arithmetic was asked, "How many bulls' tails to the moon?" to which he replied, "One, if it's long enough." Is it possible for something to add up to more than it is? Is it possible for something to add up to less than it is? Is it possible to count pearls and oysters together? Is it possible for the sum of parts of something to be less than the whole of that something?

Can obscenity be defined in terms of body language?

What oil company sponsors the sounds from a seashell?

What are onomatopoeic sounds really like? Define them as they should be.

What is Optimism as Voltaire has Pangloss define it?

Discuss the fact that Oriental definitions reach their limits hardly before they have begun. Do these limits of definition limit, as well, the thing(s) defined?

What is omitted in Oriental painting? Is the omission a fault? Does it change the definition of what painting in general is?

"Paint what you know is there, not what you see," said Gertrude Stein in reference to cubism. Define what is meant by her statement.

Write a definition of what one might see in a photograph that is contrived to be confusing.

Write a definition showing that plain talk is the hardest kind of oral expression.

Write a definition of pleasure based on Aphra Behn's saying that "Variety is the soul of pleasure."

What does the pledge of allegiance mean? What do its individual words mean, especially the words *pledge*, *allegiance*, *flag*, *nation*, *indivisible*, *liberty*, *justice*, and *all*?

Everyone has a different definition for, or understanding of, the word *poetry*. There are as many different definitions for it as there are people. What is your definition of it?

Was all poetry, as the saying goes, written before time began?

A legislator said that he could get through legislation for teaching poetry in prison only if he did not call it poetry. What definition of poetry is so distrusted that legislators would not want it taught in prison?

When is progress inhumane, or does progress always, by definition, help humanity?

"A proverb is much matter decocted into few words," said Thomas Fuller.

A young boy is quoted in a newspaper item as saying that he likes radio more than television because he can "see the pictures better." What definition is at work in his seeing?

Define *reaction*. Remember that one person's reaction is not another's. There may even be many people whose knee reflexes are controlled, for example, by hitting their opposing knees.

Define *reductio ab adsurdum* to illustrate that it is an ambiguous term.

Do children define what they draw? Do they draw to reproduce, or to represent? Write a comparison/contrast definition of the terms *reproduction* and *representation*.

Show by comparison/contrast definition that *re-sign* and *resign* are opposites in meaning.

Show by comparison/contrast definition what a professor meant by saying that there was "entirely too much student rest" on campus.

Define *reverse discrimination*.

Show by definition that what is right or wrong to one person is not the same to another.

Define the "road-not-taken" syndrome.

What is a "roadrunner"? Is it, as Rod Powell says, a bird that is "still running" when some other creature might have stopped? Do definitions and names limit in this way the things they define or name?

Develop a definition of one of the seasons like this one from *Time* magazine: "Autumn: A Season for Hymning and Hawing."

What does it mean to be selfish in practice but not in principle?

What is the most important sense, according to your definition?

Illustrate unusual definitions of the senses, as in this quotation from Shakespeare: "The eye of man hath not heard, the ear of man hath not seen, man's hand is not able to taste, his tongue to conceive, nor his heart to report, what my dream was."

What is the second definition of "seven-year itch"?

A cartoon asks, "Are you shocked at the things that don't shock you anymore?" What two definitions, at least, are there of *shock* in this quotation?

Does too much shortening make you short? Ask similar questions of other words whose definitions are deceptive.

What activity do you consider to be "sick"?

A visitor to Northern Ireland was asked which side he was on in the conflict there, and he answered, "I am on the side that doesn't require that I have to be on a side." Is it possible, by definition, not to be on a side in some issue?

Sometimes the sign is not the real message, as when a welcome mat is put out just for convention or when a dictator says that he welcomes criticism. Define a sign that does not mean what it says.

A store sign announces that "everything must go." What is being sold?—Signs, in a store specializing in them. Define the lesson in this.

What is a silver spoon? Is it necessarily a good thing? To the Jews fleeing the Germans it meant death, because it represented the wealth the Nazis were envious of.

Simple things are often the hardest to define. Illustrate the point by defining a door, a two-letter word, a color, or even the words *simple* and *simplicity*.

Define the word *sin* by comparison/contrast of its definitions in Webster's Third and Webster's Second Unabridged. Why did the definitions change?

"Ignorance is not innocence but sin," said Robert Browning.

Is almost anything that is fun defined as a sin?

Define the expression, "since God knows when."

Define whether it is the sleeper, or the bed, that gets tangled.

What is the "social calendar" of the poor?

Define an animal that has a social security number.

Define a human being as a social security number.

Show how spelling confuses definition, as in the following "One, two, three, Gough!"

Discuss by definition the fact of a statue's shaking its fist at a snowy sky.

Show that stereotyping is so reckless that it sometimes gives the same solutions to opposing problems or definitions.

Define an old stereotype, such as the one that said that a 50–50 sharing in the home was this: the wife cooked, the husband ate.

Does one have to be in prison to go "stir-crazy"?

"Style is whatever makes writing distinguishable even where it is not distinguished," said W.D. Powell. What is your definition of *style*?

Define someone so lacking in subtlety as to be like the mother, say, who sent her prisoner son a buzz-saw in a huge cake.

"There is a superstition in avoiding superstition," said Sir Francis Bacon. What is your definition of *superstition*?

The "surprise package" that Hagar leaves his wife is clearly a washing pot. Do people define themselves, as Hagar does here, by their definitions of other things?

Define, in your own way, what is meant by the song title, "Ah, Sweet Mystery of Life."

Does Swiss cheese have holes to help you recognize what it is? Which comes first in a definition, the thing defined—or merely our external impression of it?

"Taste is the feminine of genius," said Edward Fitzgerald. What is taste? What is good taste? What is bad taste?

Does teamwork mean team work?

Telephone books may be used not only for locating numbers but also for standing on. Does a momentary function of a thing change that thing's definition?

Do you define television as a literal, or a symbolic, medium?

Why, by definition, can there never be a television commercial that ends unhappily?

If we didn't have television commercials to define how we live, what would we do?

If the television or radio announcer tells you to "stand by" when you're sitting, who's to know the difference?

Show how the titles of certain television shows can be used interchangeably and with reasonable accuracy.

Someone accidentally defined television as an "escape goat." How accurate is this definition, whether or not it is an intended one?

Why is a television or a radio commercial referred to as a "message"?

How would you define "the thought of God"—meaning "God's thought"?

Can anyone—such as a timekeeper "keep" time?

"The time is now . . . "—Is it possible by definition for time to be now?

"Scientists know no time," said Da Vinci. Give a definition of time as he defined it, or understood it, in this statement.

"The time is now seventeen minutes before the hour," said the disc jockey, to which a listener responded, "What hour?" What two definitions of time are seen here?

What is the difference in definition between *time* and *eternity*?

How would a prisoner probably define *time*?

Time and distance are irrelevant, it is said, to the Latin. How do Americans feel about time and distance?

Define what Lord Byron meant by referring to Time as the "Avenger."

They really do say "All aboard!" What other truths are often defined almost as if they were clichés?

A prisoner is asked what comes after five and says "ten years to life." A time keeper might have said "5:01." A sophisticate might have said "cocktails." A stock broker might have said "5 1/8." Consider different ways time is defined depending on the person defining it.

Is the term *totalitarianism* applied only to communism?

How is the tourist's view of a foreign locale defined?

Define *translation*. Myles NaGopaleen, the Irish journalist, said of it: "If I write in Irish what I conceive to be 'Last Tuesday was very wet,' I like to feel reasonably sure that what I've written does not in fact mean 'Mr. so-and-so is a thief and a drunkard.' "

Regarding translation of the Bible there is the contention of some that angels were symbolic of, rather than literal evocations of, messengers from God. How does definition affect translation?

Define some confused translations caused by computers, especially in their identification of the sexes. Some computers, for example, have made men pregnant.

"We forgive you for trespassing against us," says a church sign, "but you still will be towed away." What vastly different definitions are there of *trespassing*?

"He said true things, but called them by wrong names," said Robert Browning.

"Truth, when witty, is the wittiest of all things," said Julius and Augustus Hare.

How would you define what an "unaskable question" is?

What does "understanding" mean when we understand people but not their handwriting?

"The universe is neither hostile nor friendly; it is merely indifferent," said John Haynes Holmes. Do you define the universe, in part, that way?

Define what is meant by the unspeakable or the unthinkable.

Is an "upset victory" a victory that upsets the victor?

"One man's vulgarity is another man's lyric," a newspaper item said of the right of Nazis to march. Discuss this fact about definition.

Sports announcer Jack Whitaker said for a U.S. Open Tennis Championship, "I hope the weather stays well." Is it possible to define the weather as something measured in terms of its health?

Hilaire Belloc said: "Strong Brother in God, and last Companion: Wine." Define or explain his definition of wine.

"We thought that he was everything/To make us wish that we were in his place," said Edwin Arlington Robinson of Richard Cory. How is a wish a definition?

Writing to Santa Claus, Charlie Brown said, " 'Tis the season to be wishy-washy." Define *wishy-washy* in this context.

Is a word a thought, or is it merely a reference point for one?

What are some words that can do quadruple duty?

RESEARCH AND REPORT

What Research-and-Report Writing Is

Research-and-report writing is nearly always formal and scholarly. Sources, both primary and secondary (from research in private papers, personal correspondence, verbal reminiscences, and so forth), are usually cited in footnotes and in a bibliography. In some cases strict formats are required. The mode of expression is basically expository, though other stylistic and rhetorical devices may certainly be used.

How to Write From Research

Effective research-and-report writing is almost impossible without clear and accurate notes. All sources should be investigated scrupulously, reported precisely, and interpreted judiciously. A disciplined effort should be made always to give credit where it is due and to see every idea, circumstance, and argument in the round. That kind of discipline is essential to good scholarship. This does not mean, however, that research-and-report writing has to be pedantic or dry. It can be as vigorous and imaginative and fulfilling as any other kind of writing. A scholarly exploration, for example, into the assassination of Becket might lead the researcher to wonder how the historical Thomas à Becket he or she discovers shapes up against the more literary Becket T.S. Eliot offers us, or Jean Anouilh. Using footnotes or not, the scholar who is gripped by such

a comparison is already breaking some fecund ground.

Locating Subjects for Research-and-Report Writing

As implied above, research-and-report writing may simply be an exposition of the information gathered on a certain subject, or it may seek to interrogate, interpret, or theorize upon that information. The subjects listed here are mostly of the information gathering variety, but, as one can see from the example of Thomas à Becket, many students will be able to take flight from almost any one of them.

This section, too, is readily informed with ideas from other parts of this book. For example, one has barely to approach a random topic listed here, "A Medieval Heretic," say, before one is into the area of definition. What is a heretic? Or, more concretely, what were some of the ideas which the 12th-Century Christian Church viewed as heretical? Was the Church right to condemn Peter Abelard as a heretic for ideas it later adopted from the pen of Thomas Aquinas? Suddenly we are into argumentation. Perhaps we can understand Abelard and his times better if we contrast him as a man and a thinker with his orthodox persecutor, Bernard of Clairvaux. They call Bernard a saint, Abelard a heretic. Before we know it we are using every stylistic device and discipline we can muster to explore what amounts to a world of difference. Or does it?

Individual Personalities

Aaron: A Second Moses?
Abdication of a Famous Royal Figure
Abigail Adams: Second First Lady
John Adams and the Boston Massacre Trial
Maude Adams: The First Peter Pan
Jane Addams and Hull House
Adenauer's Stand Against Hitler
Adrian I and Charlemagne
Aesop: The Teller of Tales
Agassiz and Glaciation
King Albert's Stand Against the Germans (World War II)
Prince Albert: Consort of Queen Victoria
John Alden: Beyond the Legend
Alexander's Last Battle
Alfred the Great as Educator
Ethan Allan
Amundsen: A Report of One of His Expeditions
Hans Christian Andersen: The Teller Not the Tales
Marian Anderson and Song
John André in the American Revolution
Susan B. Anthony and Suffrage
Chester Alan Arthur: His Quarrel with President Hayes
The Real King Arthur
An Arctic or Antarctic Journey
The First Astronomer
Attila the Hun
Crispus Attucks
John James Audubon
Marcus Aurelius
Jane Austen of the Small Town
Bach: His Occupation Not as a Composer
Francis Bacon's Legal Problems
Balboa as Discoverer
The Veep: Alben Barkley
P.T. Barnum as a Showman
Ethel Barrymore on Stage
Clara Barton and The Red Cross
Judge Roy Bean and "The Law West of the Pecos"
Becket's Assassination
Alexander Graham Bell as a Teacher
Bernadette of Lourdes
Bernhardt's First American Tour
Bismarck's Unification of Germany
Elizabeth Blackwell, First Woman Doctor of the
    United States
Captain Bligh and the *Bounty*
Queen Anne Boleyn
Bolívar's Unsuccessful Beginnings
Boone and the Cumberland Gap

Lucrezia Borgia: All Evil?
Was There a *Good* Borgia?
Gutzon Borglum
Omar Bradley
Matthew Brady, Civil War Photographer
Willy Brandt: More Than a Mayor
Just Nicholas Breakspear, Not Adrian IV
The Death of John Brown
Robert Bruce's Persistence
Bryan as Perpetual Candidate
Ralph Bunche and the United Nations
Edmund Burke in Support of Revolution
Aaron Burr and Alexander Hamilton
Byron's Last Days
Augustus Caesar
How Caligula Became Emperor
Andrew Carnegie as Philanthropist
Carver as a Scientist
Casement's Death, Burial, and Reburial
Castro as Revolutionary
Catherine the Great
William Caxton
The Fall of Neville Chamberlain
Neville Chamberlain's Treaty with Hitler
Chiang Kai-shek and Formosa
How did Chiang Kai-shek Rise to Power?
Churchill's Loss of the Prime Ministry
Cicero as Orator
El Cid: But What Did He *Do*?
Clemenceau as Peace Negotiator
George M. Cohan, Showman
Joseph Conrad's Self-Teaching
Coolidge and the Boston Police Strike
Copernicus and His Theory
Charlotte Corday
Cortez and Montezuma
Stephen Crane's Sea Rescue
A Great Criminal Reformer
The Fall of *Richard* Cromwell, Oliver's Son
Madame Curie Before She Was Madame Curie
Currier and Ives
Salvador Dali's Art
The Public Personality of Salvador Dali
Richard Henry Dana and the Change of Naval Laws
Darwin and *The Beagle*
The Dauphin
The Trial of Jefferson Davis
Charles Dickens and Prison
Diderot and the Encyclopedia
Babe Didrikson
The Pardon of Dreyfus

Isadora Duncan
Edward the Confessor in 1066
The First Queen Elizabeth
The Second Queen Elizabeth
Erasmus and Thomas More
Mary Ann Evans *alias* George Eliot
The Empress Eugénie
Guy Fawkes and the Gunpowder Plot
Edward Fitzgerald as Translator
Henry Ford and the Assembly Line
George Fox and the Quakers
Franco as a Soldier
Anne Frank and Her Diary
"Fulton's Folly"
Galen and Astronomy
Galileo's Troubles
Gandhi and Pacifism
William Lloyd Garrison
Geronimo in Old Age
Lillian and Dorothy Gish
Gordon at Khartoum
Grant and Lee at Appomattox
Grant's Troubles as President
The Nine-Day Reign of Lady Jane Grey
Zane Grey's Writing Success
D.W. Griffith and the Making of *The Birth of a Nation*
Haakon VII, King of Norway
Hadrian the Builder
Dag Hammarskjold
Hannibal and the Alps
Harold Godwin, 1066
Hawkins and the *Armada*
Hawthorne's Ancestor at Salem
How Hayes Won the Presidency
Hemingway as a Young Journalist
Henry VIII's First Wife
O. Henry's Latin American Experience
A Medieval Heretic
Hindenburg and Hitler
Hippocrates
Hirohito: Merely a Figurehead?
Hiss and Whittaker Chambers
A Historian from Modern Times
The Hohenzollern Family
Hans Holbein
Hal Holbrook
Oliver Wendell Holmes, Jr.
Who Was Homer?
Why Hoover Lost the Presidency
J. Edgar Hoover's Popularity Decline
Sam Houston as Governor

Howe's Patent Difficulties
Julia Ward Howe
W.D. Howells, "Father" of American Literary Realism
Charles Evans Hughes as a Presidential Candidate
Anne Hutchinson as a Religious Leader
The Huxleys
Ibsen and Censorship
Mr. Inside and Mr. Outside of Football
Ivan the Terrible
Stonewall Jackson Before the American Civil War
King James I: Coming Into Power
Thomas Jefferson as Inventor
Thomas Jefferson as Naturalist
Thomas Jefferson as Translator
Thomas Jefferson as Writer
Edward Jenner
Joan of Arc in Battle
King John and the *Magna Carta*
Andrew Johnson's Stormy Presidency
Samuel Johnson's *Dictionary*
Joshua and the Battle of Jericho
Juarez, the Lincoln of Mexico
Judith and Holofernes
Keats in Italy
Helen Keller as a World Figure
Jerome Kern
Khrushchev in America
Captain Kidd
The Krupp Family
Mayor LaGuardia
Lao-Tse
Lenin's Tomb
Leonardo da Vinci
Lewis and Clark Expedition
Ben Lilly and Theodore Roosevelt
Lincoln as a Congressman
Livingstone's Contributions to Africa
Louis XIV
Toussaint L'Ouverture
Magellan's Circumnavigation
Sir Thomas Malory
Manet
Horace Mann
How Did Mao Rise to Power?
Queen Maria Theresa
Melville in Typee
Mesmer and Hypnotism
Mirabeau—A Nobleman for the People
An Authority on Molluska
Monet
James Monroe and the Era of Good Feeling

Zero Mostel
The Childhood Genius of Mozart
A Figure Behind the Scenes in the Movie World
Carry Nation's War Against Drink
Nefertiti, Egyptian Queen
Nero and the Burning of Rome
The Last Czar Nicholas
Florence Nightingale
Alfred Nobel and the Nobel Prizes
The O'Higgins Family of Chile
Mungo Park, Explorer of the Niger
The Fall of Parnell
Pasteur Before His Discoveries
Robert Peel and the Bobbies
Samuel Pepys and His Diary
Frances Perkins, First Woman Cabinet Member
Pershing and Pancho Villa
Petain in the Second World War
Peter the Great
Philip II of Macedon
King Philip of Spain
The Piccard Brothers and Underwater Exploration
Pickett's Charge
The Plantaganets
Poe at West Point
Polk's Acquisition of California
Polk: Why Is He Considered One of Our Great Presidents?
Marco Polo in China
Katherine Anne Porter in Mexico
Wiley Post
An Obscure President
_____ Before the Presidency
_____ After the Presidency
Serge Prokofiev
Pythagoras
Rapp the Harmonist
Robespierre and the Reign of Terror
Will Rogers and Congress
Will Rogers and the Presidency
Eleanor Roosevelt as a Public Figure
Franklin Roosevelt's First Term
Teddy Roosevelt's Failed Campaign for the Presidency
José San Martín's Last Revolution
George Bernard Shaw's Alphabet
Sitting Bull
Death of Socrates
DeStalinization of Russian History
Robert Louis Stevenson on Samoa
Harriet Beecher Stowe and the American Civil War
The Phenomenon of Shirley Temple
Margaret Thatcher's Political Career

Arnold Toynbee
The Mystery of B. Traven, Author
Truman's First Weeks as President
Queen Victoria's Diamond Jubilee
Booker T. Washington
Young Washington's Military Defeats
James Watt
George Westinghouse and Transportation
Simon Wiesenthal: Hunter of Men
Oscar Wilde in America
The First King William of England
Wilson's Wife as Acting President
Xerxes Examined
Zapata as a Revolutionary
Zola in Support of Dreyfus

Places, Events, Conditions

Aberdeen Shipping
Acapulco Tourism
Aegean Islands and Early Civilization
The Aegean Sea and Early Commerce
The Climate of Africa
The Purchase of Alaska
Alexandria, Egypt
Alsace-Lorraine and World War I
Recent Amazon Exploration
Travel on the Amazon
Andersonville Prison
The Central Andes
Peruvian Andes
Annapolis and Education
Human Life in Antarctica
Arden Forest
Atlantic City and Gambling
Atlantis: What Do We Know of It?
The Australian Outback
From Austria-Hungary to Austria and Hungary
The Government of Barbados
Basel As a 15th-Century Religious Center
Bath, England, During the 14th Century
The Belgian Congo
The Government of Belize
Bergen, Norway
The Black Hole of Calcutta
Bombay and Commerce
Brasilia: The Foundation
Britain As It Appeared to the Roman Conquerors
Buckingham Palace
Chesapeake Bay
The Congo and "Civilization"

Constantinople to Istanbul
Costa Rican Government: The Most Stable in Latin America?
Devil's Island
Down Under
The Kingdom of East Anglia
Easter Island: Its Care and Operation
El Salvador Population Problem
The Equator of Ecuador
The Faeroe Islands
The Falkland Islands: The Quarrel Over Their Ownership
Fiji Islands and Progress
The Government of French Guiana
Mt. Fujiyama and Religion
The Government of Finland
Flanders and the Flemish Language
Florida Keys
Florida of the Past
The Gadsden Purchase
Administering the Galapagos Islands
Giant's Causeway
Granada as a Separate Country in Spain
The Great Divide
Great Lakes Shipping
Guadalajara Architecture
Guam and the Military
The Government of the Hague
The Unity of Hawaii
Helsinki
The Heptarchy of England
The Himalayas
Hollywood: The First Year
Indigenous Honduras
Hong Kong
Volcanoes of Iceland
The Intracoastal Waterway of the Atlantic Coast
Volcán Irazú
Isle of Man
Problems of Tourists in Jamaica
Japanese Economy
Japanese Government During American Occupation
Klondike
The Political Status of Labrador
Liechtenstein
Lithuania and Russian Relations
London and Taxation
Luxembourg
Machu Picchu
Mammoth Cave of Kentucky
The Mississippi River During the Civil War
Montreal and Its Two Major Languages

Colonization of the Moon
Mount Rainier as a Training Center
Mt. St. Helens
Makeup of the Netherlands
Nevada: Not Just Divorce and Gambling
New Zealand Government
New Zealand Topography
Nicaragua and Earthquake Recovery
Nicaragua and Political Corruption
Northwest Territories and the Royal Canadian Mounted Police
Norway and Neutrality
Inhabitants of Nova Scotia
Habitat of Okefenokee Swamp
The Founding of "Old Town" in _____
The Papal States
The Petrified Forest of Arizona
Philippine Government Since World War II
Poland as a Satellite
Puerto Rico: What Is Its Political Status?
Puget Sound: Steps Towards Ecological Control
Quito, Ecuador: Two Cities in One
Rhode Island: Is There Anything Big There?
The Mystery of Roanoke Island
Sumatra
Wales: Its Origins
The Yukon and Adventure
Government of Zaire
Zurich as Center of the Reformation

World Peoples, Ancient and Modern

The Acadian People
The Aleuts
American Indian Tribal Organization
The 19th-Century Apache
The Arabian Nomad
The Basques: A People Apart
The Celts: An Unassimilable People
Central American Indians
The Civilization at Chichen-Itzá
The Druids and Sun Worship
Ebla People, 2400-2250 BC
The Last of the Etruscans
A European People in Argentina
Evidences of Early Man in the Bering Strait
The Hittites
The Hopi Indian
Huns
The Iberi People
The Incas

Who Were the Indo-Europeans?
Mayan Civilization
Pueblo Indians
Stonehenge
The Tarahumaras
The Tasaday Indians: Then as Now
What Civilization Was at Tikal?
The Visigoths
The Walloons

War, Political Strife, Wartime Conditions and Operations

The Admiralty of Great Britain During World War II
The Battle of Agincourt
The "Alabama Claims"
After the Famous Battle of the Alamo
American Expeditionary Force
American Neutrality in World War II
The Battle of Antietam
Bacon's Rebellion
Barcelona and the Spanish Civil War
Anti-Aircraft Defense During the Battle of Britain
Blackouts During World War II
A Famous Blockade
The Boer War
The Boxer Rebellion
Burma Death March
The CIA: Its Early Operation
Cavalry of the Middle Ages
Cambodian Blood Purges, 1970s
The Cheyenne Wars
Coxey's Army
Dachau During World War II
Delaware During the Civil War
The First Democratic Struggle
Desertion During Wartime
Dunkirk (Dunquerque) During World War II
"Fifty-four Forty or Fight"
The French and Indian War
French Revolution: The Bastille
Galveston in War Defense
What Happened at Guernica?
Battle of Hastings
Hiroshima
Holy Alliance
The Hundred Years' War
Hungarian Revolution, 1956
British Intelligence Operations During World War I
Ireland: The Easter Uprising
Occupation of Ethiopia by Italy
War of Jenkins' Ear

Battle of Jutland
A Famous Liberation Struggle
The *Lusitania*
The Mercenary Soldier of Early Times
The Mexican War
Militia Children/Post-Viet Nam Stress Syndrome
Revival of the Nazis
Non-Communists in Chile
The October Revolution
The Office of Price Administration
Paraguay and the Gran Chaco
Pearl Harbor: What Did the Americans Know Before?
Potsdam Agreement
Prisoner-of-War Agreements
The Six-Day War
The Soccer War
Soldiers as Viewed by Walter Bagehot
Taiwan and Mainland China
Andrew Jackson and the Vale of Tears
Radio and World War II
Yalta: What Happened There?
Yokohama

Philosophical, Political, and Religious Groups or Movements

The John Birch Society: Where and How Is It Now?
What Was Bolshevism?
The Brook Farm Experiment
Christianity Comes to _____ (Ireland, England, or the United States)
Christianity 100 AD
The Greek Origin of Democracy
Ecumenical Government
Early Feminism
The Decline of Feudalism
The Geneva Convention
The Greenback Party
Islamic Fundamentalism
Early References to Jesus, Mohammad, and Buddha Not in Religious Books
Is the Concept of Liberty New?
Where Does the Idea of a Constitution Originate?
The MacDowell Colony
Marriage and Courtship in _____
Monogamy and Polygamy in Religious Groups
Old-Time Religion, BC
Polygamy
Supreme Court and FDR
Underground Railroad
UNESCO

Non-Human Creature Life

The Aardvark/The Aardwolf
The Albatross
An Amphibious Creature
The Anaconda
The Ant Colony
Appaloosa
The Baboon
The Badger in Defense
The Barracuda
The Bear in Hibernation
The Beaver's Engineering Skills
Bird Migration
A Bird Type
The Boar
The Boll Weevil and Cotton
Canadian Wild Goose
The Chachalaca Bird
The Dingo of Australia
The Exciting Life of the Earthworm
Everglades Bird Life
Flamingo
The Guidance System of _____ (a certain insect, bird, or reptile)
Hornbill
Hummingbird
Insect Colonies
Kangaroo
King Snake
Minnows as Mosquito Controls
The Migration and Survival of the Mysterious Monarch Butterfly
The Mongoose
The Nest of the _____
Oyster Beds
The Piranha
The Pterodactyl
Salamander
The Truth About Sharks
Squid
Eating Habits of the Whale

Language-Related Subjects

Origin of the English Alphabet
A Study of a Single Letter in the English Alphabet
Origin of Anglo-Saxon
The Major Periods of English Language Change
Esperanto, World Language
On "Passing Away," "Expectorating," and "Issuing Forth"—A Study of Victorian Euphemisms

The Language of Hawaii
Icelandic Language
Indo-European Language
A New Language in the Old
The State of the Language at the Time of the American Revolution
Language on the Island of Skye

Medical Subjects

Acupuncture
Alchemy
The First Anesthetic
The Artificial Heart
Aspirin
Autism
Extraterrestrial Biology
Cause of the Black Death
Contamination
Danger Symptoms of _____
Dermatology
Eyes in the Back of the Head
General Health
Heart Disease(s)
Successful Heart Transplanting
The Unknown in Human Behavior
Hypnotism
Inoculation
Mental Illness
Out-of-Body Experiences
Quack Medicine
Research in Senility
Sickle Cell Anemia
Sleepwalking
X-Ray Dangers

Inventions, Devices, Operations

Abacus
Agricultural Machinery
Air Vessels Before the Plane
The First Bathysphere
The Gutenberg Press
The First Automobile
Sikorsky's Helicopter
The *Hindenburg* Airship
The Cosmotron
Submarine
Rocket Launch
Automobile Brakes
The Ultimate Weapon
Use of X-Rays in the Oil Industry

Natural Phenomena

The Results of Glaciation
Gravity: What It Is, How It Works
The Gulf Stream
Holes in Space
Eye of the Hurricane
Icebergs
Magnetism
Moon Mysteries
Outer-Space Life
Saturn
Seasons
The Truth About Snowflakes
Sunspots
Winds
Zephyr

Written Media, Special Books

Consumer Complaints Through Newspaper Columns
Early Egyptian Almanacs
Poor Richard's Almanack
Publishing: The Creation of Best Sellers
Early Translation of the Bible
Book Design
The First Book
The Change of the Calendar to Its Present Form
The Egyptian Calendar
The Roman Calendar
The Dead Sea Scrolls
Hornbook
Library of Congress
Translation(s) of the New Testament
Pulitzer Prizes: Origin and Definition
Talking Books for the Blind

Education

The First Academy: Plato's School
Teaching in the Alaskan Wilderness
Chautauqua and Early Education
Cherokee Education
The Entertainer as Educator: Medieval Minstrels,
    Scops, and Troubadours
Correctional Systems for Juvenile Delinquents
Knighthood Training
Medieval Monks and Education
Oxford—The College System
The Founding of the First American University
Recruiting of University Athletes
The Founding of West Point
Xerxes Did Die: A Study of Early American Education

Professions, Occupations, Employment

Air Traffic Control
The Boat People of the Orient
Canadian Fishermen
The Canadian Mounted Police
Civilian Conservation Corps
Eskimo Occupations
The Industrial and Professional Role of Women During
    World War II
Market Week in _____
Mining in Chile
The Operation of an Ocean Liner
Peonage
Seafolk of the Sub-Arctic
American Seaman/Seawoman Occupations
Siberian Occupations
The U.S. Mint System
Unemployment in History
The WPA
Xerox Company Competitors

Human-Made Constructions and Designs

The Alcan Highway
The Building of the Alhambra
The First American East-West Trains
Pressed-Metal Ornamentation in Architecture
The Atlantic Cable
The Tower of Babel
The Battle Helmet in _____
The Bayeaux Tapestry
Bell Founding
The Mystery of Bridge Building
Testing Bridge Strengths
Canal-Building
Cathedrals of Sir Christopher Wren
Covered Wagon
The Crystal Palace of Queen Victoria
Construction of the Eiffel Tower
Elgin Marbles
Erie Canal
The Gold Museum of Bogotá
The Golden Gate
The Great Wall of China
The Hanging Gardens of Babylon
Hollywood Bowl
Making of Hoover Dam
Houston Ship Channel
The Leaning Tower of Pisa
New Mexico Fort of the 19th Century
The Panama Canal Locks

The Original Puppets
Pyramid Construction
Early Railroad Building
Jungle Railroads: Costa Rica or Panama
The Richest Street in the World
Showboats
The Stradivarius Violin
The Taj Mahal
The Trans-Canada Railroad
Tikal Pyramids: How They Are Uncovered
A Viking Boat
The Construction (or Re-Construction) of
    Westminster Abbey
World's Fair in Chicago, 1893
The Dam of the Zuider Zee

Sports, Entertainments, Recognitions

The First Automobile Race
Boogie Woogie
English Channel Swims
Greyhound Racing
The Hall of Fame: Its Operation
Hockey
Indian Dance
The Kentucky Derby
The Triple Crown
Yacht Racing

Sciences, Studies, Skills, Inquiries, Observations of the Universe

Acoustics
Aerial Photography
Determining the Age of the Earth
Anthropology: One Way of Studying the History of
    Humanity
Timing the Ages of Humanity by Archaeology
The Use of Astronomy to Measure Time
Research in Egyptology
Fingerprinting
Futuristics
Tracing Genealogy
Hieroglyphics
Hymnology
Oceanography
Paleontology
Psychology (Psychoanalysis) and Nursery Rhymes
Telepathy
Worship of the Heavens

Flora and Derivatives

The Big Thicket of Texas
The Black Forest

Cocoa
Cotton History
Cranberries
Dandelions
The Ginseng Plant
Protection of Crops Without Insecticides

Media and Media Events

The Abbey Theatre of Dublin
The Academy Awards
Early Advertising Slogans That Have Survived
The First Advertising
Amateur Filmmaking
Cannes Film Festival
How the Comics Began
Life Magazine and Photography
One Hundred Years of Headlines
Twenty-Five Years of Public Television
The Origin of Radio Broadcasting in the United States
The First Photography
Early Radio Technique
Quiz Show Scandals
The $64,000 Question
Subliminal Advertising
Orson Welles' Report of an "Invasion," October 30, 1938
Yellow Journalism
Famous Hoaxes

Miscellaneous

The Aa Rivers
Absorption and Osmosis
The Complex Adoption Procedure
The Albany Congress
The Alien and Sedition Laws
How to Become an American Citizen
Chronological History of Integration in America
Annexation of Territory
April Fools' Day
"Arctic Hysteria"
Arlington Cemetery
Sales of Autographs
The Aztec Priest
The Case That Ended Blacklisting on Television
Carpetbaggers
Caviar
A Cheese Type
Chic Europe: Mainly American?
Is There Consciousness Before Birth?
Ancient Cosmetics
Criminal Reform

The Deirdre Legend
What Outlook for Democracy in Argentina?
Can You Spare a Dime?—The Conditions of the Average
    Citizen During the Depression
Divorce Among Royal Members
The Welsh *Eisteddfod*
Emancipation Proclamation
The Belief in the "Evil Eye"
The Fair Deal
History of Fasting
Fata Morgana
Ancient Financial Credit
The First Labor Union
The Get-Rich Quick Schemes
Great Lakes
The Origin of Hallowe'en
Heraldry
Holy Roman Empire
House of Commons, House of Lords
The Huguenots
The Ice Age
Care of Illegitimate Children
The Industrial Revolution
Inheritance Taxes
The Iron Age
The Italian Renaissance
Juvenile Court
The Know-Nothings
Law Enforcement
A Legal System in Elizabethan Times for Protecting
    the Writer

The Longest Wait
The Beginning of Marriage-Ceremony Traditions
May Day
Small States—Israel, Athens, Florence, Elizabethan
    England—as Great Influences
The New Copyright Laws
The New Deal
Nuremberg Trials
The Historical Limits of America's Open Door Policy
Paintings as History
The Canadian Parliament
The Parliament of India
Popular Songs During the Civil War
Culture During the Restoration Period
How Does/Did Royalty View Commoners?
Runaways
Salem Witchcraft Trials
San Francisco Conference
Seven: The Magic Number of the Ancients
Snake Worship
The Spanish Inquisition
The State Lottery
U.S. Aid
Voodooism in Haiti
Voting Rights of Blacks in the Post-Civil-War South
Women's Suffrage Fights in Great Britain
What We Know About Ourselves
World Trade
Yugoslavia After Tito
The Ancient Yule
The Zambezi River

CREATIVE WRITING

What Creative Writing Is

Creative writing is essentially imaginative. It most often takes the form of drama, fiction, or poetry (including songs). But given that imaginative reach, along with the language tools and techniques needed to realize it, any form of writing discussed in this book can become creative. One might call this type of writing *full-blooded*—nourished, as it must be, with an abundance of heart.

How to Write Creatively

In this type of writing, following a format can cramp a writer's style. At bottom, there is no way one can tell another person *how* to write creatively. Probably no teacher can do much more than inspire the student with a quality set of rhetorical tools, an open atmosphere, a love of language, and a sense of possibility, then let the newborn beast have its head and hope for the best.

The natural element of creative writing is freedom. This is the place to let go, to let the student *be*. Of course that does not mean that the teacher abandons any new writer to a miasma of self-indulgence. Rather, the student should be guided and encouraged through the certain failures, through try after try and endless errors and those very few quiet triumphs, until he or she begins to realize that dreams can indeed come alive, take shape and grow, stand full and real as any creature of bone, flesh, blood.

Here again is where we call up every writing mode and device we can think of—not only the modes touched upon in this book, but other more literary devices as well. We bring to bear the full force of metaphor, alliteration, repetition, rhyme, rhythm, meter, and so on—all with the understanding that nothing is sacred if it holds the student back from creative expression. It can be instructive and fun simply to experiment with such devices. But in the end they will probably be used less for their own sake than because they are evoked, often mysteriously, called up out of the material itself, whatever it may be.

So it is indeed clear that this is not the time to worry too much about sentence fragments, erratic punctuation, or many of the other grammatical elements that must necessarily concern us in more formal types of composition. There is at least one handy rule-of-thumb for creative writing: If it works, use it.

Locating Subjects for Creative Writing

The subjects listed in this section do not pretend to be anything more than suggestions, ideas for approaching various forms of creative writing. They could inspire almost anything—a play, a story, a poem or song, a character sketch, a writing experiment. It hardly matters. More important than the image or idea is the imagination it fires.

It is in many ways apparent from the above that any section in this book may be used to fire that creative imagination. Special attention might well be paid, though, to the chapters on narrative and description. Some narrative element is often important, even essential, in creative writing. Crafting more or less footloose material to the demands of a narrative line, making it fit, making it belong, can lift a common piece of descriptive or expository writing towards something larger, give it form, harmony—turn it, that is to say, towards art.

Brainstorming Fictional Themes

me and the computer
memories of smoke
memories in smoke
one more, too many
due unto others
transients eating around a campfire
deprivation of the mind
smashing taboos
knowing how to keep company away from the door
living on borrowed time
moving in reverse into the future
vowing a new fight
toughest break
expectations fulfilled/unfulfilled
a decent interval
mislaid values
tar-and-feathering
losing battle(s)
still not enough
daring/not daring to do
second chance
on solid ground
duplication(s)
at the corner store
something due
expecting the unexpected
marking the spot
a tinkling cymbal
the forgotten year/hour/day
prisoner at home
any reasonable offer
suspension/suspense
new world
a goodbye to Smithville
final questions of commencement
seizing the day
open to suggestions
trying to hold on
not able to face it
carrying on
impetuosity
repeating history
in the interim
hocus pocus
head over heels
bankruptcy
life in TV commercials
frustration(s) of the final hour
being tempted to do something one doesn't want to do

dehumanization of sex
searching for Atlantis
holocaust
promise, no delivery
born every minute
repository of records found 1000 years from now
never made public until now
the perfect arrangement
best in the West
acquiring a new name
an old (or ancient) mystery solved
unrecognized, unrewarded
short reflection(s), long ideas
private hall of fame of local characters
Et tu, Brute?
surprising finds about one's ancestry
the death or decline of _____
walking away from the impossible
out o' sight
a historian of the _____ building
the last challenge
admitting the truth at last
seeing the light
my own crystal ball
third chance
witness to _____
making history
monkey business
tourist trap
walking tall/walking short
individualism as defined in the future
being told to leave home
junkyard jamboree
whitewashing
backfire of ploy
lights, camera, action
asylum for the reputedly sane
beyond the limits
the dignity of independence
recognition at last
switching over
challenge of the spirit
unauthorized biography
oversympathetic, considering what happened
the real beginnings of humanity
not by choice
the white(d) sepulchre
early responsibilities
bitter truth(s)
just between friends
mission/vision accomplished

brief encounter(s)
a voice still heard
controlling destiny
cabbages and kings
memoirs
easy way out
the price of glory
best rival, best friend
last refuge
too awed to do anything about it
long-distance dating
giving away secrets
keeping secrets
those forgotten by time
afraid to let go/afraid not to let go
still at large
born exile
all shook up
darkness my old friend
behind the wheel/behind the eightball
shadow-boxing
armed and dangerous
history as it happens
heaven-sent
no closed doors
unwanted
Andrew Jackson's famous duel
curiosity about _____
the wrong person
secret life/double life/secret lives
war between _____ and _____
rescue squad
_____'s mad idea
my Oedipus complex
a report from _____
the last hurrah
the last fling
looking backward and forward
the secret word
discovery of the first wheel
discovery of fire
discovery of speech
stay of execution
forgone but not forgotten
before I was five
due to circumstances beyond our control
conversation about a movie, a book, a show on television
going forward
the self-same hill (from a poem by John Milton)
disowned, disinherited
disappearing ships, planes, persons

when I was old
surrendering
hunkering down
mugging a mugger
bystander
returning
king of the hill
short but glorious career
hair on end
but waking up
sour grapes
lifeline
the flesh and the spirit
long journey, bad roads
marked man/woman
unsigned
riders to the sea
witch watch
parents and children
itinerary through the mind
seeking a long-lost relative
first sighting
putting a tail on someone, as in a spy movie
edging along
the three strangers
if I were not alive
a thousand miles of mountain road, a thousand miles of desert sand
conversation between clerks in a department store
going backward
taking the plunge
doing what is expected of you, not doing what is expected of you
covering an escape
letting off steam
bother/bothering
the beginning of consciousness
the learning tree
captive of time
bull ring
the search for a missing letter, notebook, diary, etc.
out of Dante
for auld lang syne
the wrong connection
a moment's surrender
leaving behind what one did not have in the first place
cross-conversation confusing the main point
family reunion requiring introductions
Melchior's telling about following the star
words, thoughts, and feelings of the first people on earth
ancient astronauts

the road to _____

morally right, legally wrong

night in a _____

not even for money

a highwayman

conversation in a barber shop or a beauty shop

for whom the bell gongs

one day late

a tortoise that lost the race

desire or will power that goes beyond death

the incredible journey

the stagedoor canteen of World War II

the ringing phone

overnight

returning home after many generations away

first theme

a rock speaking of its history

a hobo insulted by someone who doesn't like his dress, his manner, or his dog

prehistoric hunt

consequence of someone's not reading a letter in time

a dream of someone who helps carry the crucifixion crosses up a hill only to find that he is to be among those to be crucified

Socratic dialogue in a fictional piece

appointment/date/liaison

account by a prisoner of the last day in a concentration camp, after the Germans had fled

conditions of an island prison

having a party of one

paradise lost/regained

a friendly relationship between a millionaire and his/her chauffeur

gold fever

trouble between the weatherman and the movie critic on the TV news

money in the mattress

sibling against sibling

once, on the river, . . .

a "now" story

coming back to life

coming back as another person or thing

undemanding of our attention or consideration

the crazy mirror (title of a children's book)

"a dream deferred"

getting through somehow

something to win over

birds of a feather

a fascination for the abominable

on any door

the switch/the sting

passing quietly through

a child's long train trip while unattended by adults

a thousand years, a thousand days

falling in love against one's will

awake in the dark

prolonged attack(s)

without benefit of clergy

competition among backwoods religious types—perhaps in the form of shouting amens or of giving big offerings when the plate is passed around

"thee a stranger" (from Matthew 25:38)

the seasons of _____

deadlines

wheelbarrow tourists in Amazon jungle

leave cancelled

getting out after a long time

together again

going home

the first meeting in the Garden of Eden

asking the unaskable

parent talking to child

rematch

once upon a time

guests of the _____

things that set off memories

the world according to _____

silent night, lonesome night

someone at the door

as up they grew

long, dark night

an experience remembered more often than any other one

anywhere the wind blows

rites of passage—birth, first love, maturity, death

carnival of souls

a reprieve after many years of being wronged

surprise ending

rewriting a narrative poem as narrative prose

a tent meeting

a medicine show

facing a hard race

from the files

if I should die before I wake . . .

a kind of glory

futureworld

instant fame

a thankless child, as in Shakespeare's *King Lear*

snowstorm

dialogue including a portrait of someone who makes a threat to leave someone else

making the first phone call

special cruise

eternity versus the moment

out of time

omen

preaching fire and brimstone

the source of a proverb

the Mexican legend of "La Llorona"

the relationship between good fortune and ignorance

a talk with someone who has lived the history

the classical unities ignored to purpose

cameo

the reader over your shoulder

the star in a grain of dust

scenes from next (week's/month's/year's) (book/movie/
TV show)

diving for treasure, real or metaphorical

a peculiar case

maze(s)

coming in, going out

forbidden alliance

the missing piece of the jigsaw puzzle

someone in a story absorbed by a mirror, a book, or a
piece of music

a single subject treated in various ways and for different
purposes

writing a theme of a story from the theme of a poem

close to, but not a part of, nature

out of season

short stay in _____

the mind's eye

inside the universe of a snowflake

before two million years ago

behind the sealed (tomb, door, passage)

ghost story

a fable/parable for our time

a touch of class

rooms without floors

the classical unities accommodated to purpose

shaggy dog

in touch with the sublime

hunting with a camera instead of a rifle

refusing to leave the solitary places

something seen in early England by one of Caesar's
legends

the Ouija board

the Will of The Wind

out past curfew

costly encounter

elementary-school burial for words and expressions such
as "ain't" and "he don't"

policeman taking a report from a witness and from the
accused

never giving up

getting to know the world by window-washing

making a deal

link with eternity

wandering all our ways (phrase from Sir Walter Raleigh)

just an act, not the real thing

a proverb refuted

unraveling lies

foundling at the doorstep

legend of the Blarney Stone

no room at the inn

the writings and thoughts of an indigenous person

a feeling of place

a mosaic tying everything together

friendship between human and animal

an hour in an hourglass: its universe

looking at what _____ has done/is doing

something seen on the road

standing on the head

interest in the news

local witches

born into the same life again

eccentric person who saves up fried eggs to serve at a
later date

misunderstanding causing humorous results in a foreign
country

Questions, Titles, Assignments, and Brainstormers for the Short Story, Novel, Novella, and Fiction Sketch

Write as if you were someone else, someone who has had
an experience in a ghetto, say, or a prisoner-of-war
camp.

Excuse Me, Lord—title for story of misguidedly religious
child.

The End Zone is Near!

Step right over here, folks!

Such love, so well-expressed, is rather unusual in these
times.

_____ is paradise enough.

Fictionalize an event as seen by different eyes' views, for
example, by a detective, a small child, a judge, a newspaper, a scandal sheet.

Doesn't anyone stay in one place any more?

Begin a story with the picture of a family walking along
the dusty road during the Depression. The mother
and father have a pole which they are carrying
mounted on their shoulders; on the pole their clothes
and the clothes of their four children are drying in
the sun. Take the story wherever it goes.

How useful is a hunch?

The more problems you have, the more alive you are, it
has been said.

Imagine where humanity can go after our current
evolution.

No one escapes feeling guilty about something.

Space explorers may not find the earth inhabited on their return.

What would a space visitor to the earth most want to talk about? What would we most want to ask him/her?

Here Lies the World.

The end is nothing; the road is all.

"It is better to remain silent and appear dumb than to speak and remove all doubt."—popular proverb.

"An event has happened, upon which it is difficult to speak, and impossible to be silent."—Edmund Burke

What would you have (done, been) if you (had, had not) (graduated, gone into the service, got married)? Give a fictional answer.

What would you have done if you had been mature during World War II?

"O holy simplicity!" said John Huss the martyr while at the stake.

"I will not reason and compare; my business is to create."—William Blake

"I must create a system, or be enslaved by another man's."—William Blake

"I have a bit of FIAT in my soul,/And can myself create my little world."—Thomas Lovell Beddoes

"Any fool may write a most valuable book by chance, if he will only tell us what he heard and saw with veracity."—Thomas Gray.

"A man will turn over half a library to make one book."—Samuel Johnson.

"Who often reads, will sometimes wish to write."—George Crabbe.

"Only those who have eaten, have drunk, and have lived with a man can write his life."—paraphrased from Samuel Johnson.

"We never do anything well till we cease to think about the manner of doing it."—William Hazlitt.

"I am always at a loss to know how much to believe of my own stories."—Washington Irving.

"Read over your compositions, and where ever you meet with a passage which you think is particularly fine, strike it out."—Samuel Johnson.

In writing, it has been said, the trouble is to find the right person, the right idea; both idea and person are already there, waiting to be discovered.

Private people sometimes make news. Private lives sometimes make news.

There was little that was meaningful to me when I was very young—but that little was a lot.

What will be found in the time capsule for the year 2788?

From dust we came?

Time Stands Still.

How would you live if you had great personal wealth?

What did you miss out on when you were young?

The River Will Come, The River Will Go.

Is all well that ends well?

He was so confused he didn't know if he was going to bed or getting up.

Seeing _____ again brought back the memory of _____ .

Whatever happened to _____ ?

South Patagonia, What Have I Done to You?—title for a story of the failure to keep a self-image appropriate to one's hometown.

Write a story about the Clementine of the song.

Write a narrative of someone happy with natural learning rather than formal learning.

Write a fictional narrative about a young person having a first experience of doubt.

Write a fictional account of a young person covering up what he/she really feels.

Write about a fearful moment, such as a close call or a brush with death.

Write a narrative of someone who, failing to find a human being with whom to share his grief, turns to an animal to tell of his sorrow.

Write a tall story intended to sound convincing.

Show fictionally how a common danger brings people together.

"Where the arrow falls, bury me."—Robin Hood.

"He's rough, vicious, sneaky, and loud-mouthed," says Andy Capp the cartoon character of an acquaintance, "but there's still somethin' about him I can't take to."

In a story entitled The Common Way (or The Uncommon Way) reflect on this quotation from Hilaire Belloc: "You who have never taken a straight line and held it, nor seen strange men and remote places, you do not know what it is to have to go round by the common way."

My life is worth more than two pages. Even the first hour of my life is worth more than two pages.

Does everyone but me leave off at an early age imitating heroic individuals?

"You can't rob me," said the grocer to the young man with the gun held shakingly in his hand. "Your buddy there with you robbed me two hours ago."

Using a Gide retelling as a reference, retell a story from the Bible or from folklore.

Everyone has a novel in him/her.

Everyone has something worth talking/writing about.

Waving at the train was one of the delights of my childhood.

Trace the history of someone found alone and injured at the side of the road.

The hotel maid squinted against the coarse daylight, and, shading her eyes with a white hand spotted with huge, burnt-brown freckles, said, "Sorry, no strangers allowed here."

I (would, would not) like to look into the future.

Dip into a dictionary of folklore and write a story suggested by one of the motifs you find there.

Many things might happen between now and then.

Write a fictional narrative developed by dialogue that reveals cause-and-effect.

"My life's an open book. Time and again I have had things happen to me that belong in the pages of a best-selling novel. I will tell you about one of these earth-shaking incidents." (The writer may want to entitle this story or novel with the title of a famous book or movie. The possibilities of writing with comic irony—that is, saying humorously precisely the opposite of what is meant—should be explored.)

Getting there, not being there, was my story.

Write a progression, outline, or frame for a long narrative.

Where would you like to explore?

Find an appropriate news story in a newspaper or magazine and rewrite it as a full-bodied first-person narrative.

Take the title of a song and use it as the title of a story having the same theme. Examples: "Scarlet Ribbons"; "Autumn Leaves"; "There's a Place for Us."

The old drunk at the table bent his head to answer his own question.

Every day is (opening day/the first day/the last day).

He hesitated, then said, "No sir."

Lazily the Lord flicked dark streams at the canvas that was the beginning of Creation.

Write a story in which the sequence of events is critically important. Possible subjects: a student demonstration, a certain process in which you participated, or an important cultural or historical event.

Do Not Disturb

The truest kind of courage comes from defeating a mountainous fear.

It started with . . .

I find happiness in the simplest things.

Put together with other writers—each one taking a certain part—a novel on a certain historical incident.

Don't cry over spilt wine.

Hear That Lonesome Whistle Blow

It Happened One Night

"I want what I want when I want it."—Henry Blossom

"I do think life is very baffling. I mean, what is one to do. Sting, or live on in the hope of meeting the Queen?"—from Flann O'Brien's translation of *Insect Play*.

Human Beings and Types for Creative-Writing Subjects

fictional self-portrait

my life with Oraculus Peep the Omniscient

narrative of Thomas Jefferson's trying to decide on the wording of the Declaration of Independence

comic-satiric portrait of a hard-drinking revivalist

caricature of a character out of a famous movie or book

interview with the president (when he/she is ten years old)

narrative about someone who garners automatic respect from individuals and groups

straw man

portrait of a mugger

the hunter

Coleridge's Kubla Khan, the person (not the poem)

tomorrow's (hero/friend/enemy/stranger)

duel between Hamilton and Burr

stranger in a strange land

Harold Honeybreath

show-off

merchant

out-of-towner

God in the process of Creation—God as living character, perhaps an artist, who needs to create for fulfillment

someone who knows only penitentiary life

someone who is lucky, told about so as to suggest that more than luck is involved

someone who unknowingly reveals oneself while telling someone else's story

someone brought to life by way of a secret diary

a character from an ad

a remarkable person

Icarus (mythical or real)

the death of Socrates

a person feeling compelled to tell his/her story

a human being's first meeting with another human being

my roots

buccaneer

shadow-seeker(s)

practical joke(r)

Lord Randall, the figure in the ballad

an animal-like person

a novelistic character transplanted from the novel to a story by you

someone, real or imaginary, that the world ought to know about

someone who becomes associated both in name and behavior with what he/she does

a character from literature placed in an uncustomary context: Humpty Dumpty as a decathlon hero, for example

the widow(er) of _____

the leader of the expedition

your life as a movie (with you watching it)

gypsy in my soul

keeper(s) of the fire

martyr

dual role/multiple masks

a mother, presented as a character in a story

a legacy from _____

someone of your invention who is involved in public life, whether in politics, entertainment, military, sports, or teaching—told about in a long comic history begin-ning, "The truth about _____ has yet to be told."

characters having dialogue drawn from their separate books

Creative Language

advertising voice of a person not seen: a razor blade speaking, a toilet bowl, a cigar

a letter from jail, camp, college, army

a prize-winning essay with nothing but clichés

hackneyed proverbs rewritten with fresh language and depth

jingoism

pastoral(s)

book epigraph or dedication

The Play (on words) is the Thing

winged words

singing telegram

conversation(s) in the closet

famous people arguing with one another from their quotations on a certain issue

a parody of a superintendent telling what *curriculum* means

Spoonerism(s)

witty words

deliberate gobbledygook or double-talk

Verbs Do It/English Is for the Verbs

note found in a bottle

note found in the trash

jive talk

satire on sightings of UFO's or Bigfoot

a thank-you letter to a newspaper for helping you in your campaign

a parody of a scandal sheet

an exam spoof

the discrepancies between movie subtitles and sound tracks

useless words passed off as useful ones

writ of "habeus escapus" as if written by fleeing inmate

a letter to the editor about being ripped-off

speeches of one sentence

a narrative in which pseudo-learning shows itself by pseudo-language

a parody of self-conscious purple prose

a parody imitating the language and mannerisms suggested by the popular self-help psychology books

a parody using advertising language to sell Zen, pragma-tism, Christianity, . . .

a parody of "Rime of the Ancient Mariner"

silent language

a pompous speech by a politician, a school superinten-dent, a head of a fraternal organization, or a business executive

a report of an incident in various ways: by journalese, elaborate diction, or oversimplified expression

a parody of psychoanalytical language explaining body language

a parody of language that says nothing, used for writing a book report or book review for a book you have not read

a story, poem, or song using an invented vocabulary of nouns, verbs, adverbs, and adjectives

Write a comic-satiric advertisement for someone who sells diplomas, affidavits, references, and the like by mail. Example: "The very day you receive your medical degree as a surgeon from us you can go right to work on your Aunt Mary. If you really want to be a surgeon, don't lose another day down at the shop. There is no reasonable explanation for spending sixteen years in preparation for a profession that requires, after all, only a good, steady hand; a clean, sharp knife; and common sense."

Describe a non-Biblical scene with Biblical language.

Offer proof of Santa Claus in extremely scientific jargon.

Write a sketch showing the language of righteous indig-nation—especially to show how impressive, and therefore effective, such language can be.

Read a certain notable style of writing and parody it. You might, to begin, want to read James Thurber's parody of Henry James—"The Beast in the Dingle"—and write your own parody of James.

Choose a common subject for parody and parody some famous lines from various poets.

Read Orwell, E.B. White, Thurber, Ezra Pound, and Salinger and imitate them in their methods of moving along in their narrative writing.

Rework a number of proverbs around a certain theme. The following example is a reworking of one of the most familiar proverbs. "You can take a war to a traffic light, but you can't make it stop."

Use a comic style of writing, such as that of Laurence Sterne in *Tristram Shandy*, to characterize a scholarly student: "The name of this scholar was _____, and, though I would not wish to be quoted on the matter (for who can say whither lists the truth when it leaves the mouth of its purveyor?), it was a name that had been with the family (themselves, if the records speak truly, a distinguished line of academi-cians since their second generation—whence there is another tale that might be told, told *again*, I might have said, where precision ought to be the domain of every recorder) for generations numbering from . . . "

Song and Poetry

Spoon River epitaph

Untitled

a song of myself

a song of butterflies

a song using the theme from a folktale or an old religious book a translation of a poem into English from a second language you know

a poem in Oriental form

An Ode to My Shoestrings

Ballad of the Dark Ladie

a song of everyone

a song about a song

a song using the music of an old hymn

a song about not singing anymore

a poem about a poem that tells of something you might have thought of yourself

A New Song

the foreverness of song

a song about singing

a song with new verses consistent with the theme and form of an old ballad

a poem *not* about love/hate/beauty

Creative Writing for a Children's Audience

children and the stars

Circus at Dawn

rectangles and circles

an oversized (mansized) mole residence for human beings

a trickster story in which the trickster is tricked

a story or poem about what happens when one enters a fairy tale

a story that responds to the question, "What do you like stories to be about?"

The Private Kingdom

The Enchanted Forest

A Dog's Devotion

In the Cloud(s)

(Wo)man in the Moon

A Living Camera

a view of what happened when the world began

an experience of *deja vu*

helping God "think up" rainbows, other things for Creation

a story of a dollar

an independent excursion

a glove as a character

a mischievous cat

a monster's story (titled "Monstory") told by the monster

a fantasy in which concrete details are used

a story about a hat that has feelings and does not want to be discarded

a story about a dream house (into which one goes in order to have dreams)

a poem that responds to the question, "What do you like poems to be about?"

In the Sky

a story or poem telling how a certain Indian got his name/her name

a view of what happens when the world ends

a story or poem answering the question, "Where were you the year before you were born?"

a story or poem affirming there were, and are, unicorns

unfinished poem to complete

Saturday cartoon(s)

baskets as characters

Cricket in Pocket

a story about pencils (named Scribble, Doodle, and Scratch) who write their own stories

a story about the king of the barnyard

a story about a dream into which one can enter at will

a story or poem about a comic-strip character

The Unwise Owl

a pet's life story in a story or poem

Life of a Tumbleweed

A Legend Relived

an unconventional letter to Santa Claus

a story or poem putting fairy tale or folktale characters in unfamiliar roles

new ending, old story

unfinished story to be completed

Other Creative Exercises

Write spontaneously and without direction on one of these: dog, brick, tree, mountain stream.

See how many words you can write—without stopping, without thinking of order, without worrying about a grade—in fifteen minutes.

Write a fictional piece or a poem that severely cuts out details but still evokes a purpose.

Write a character sketch using understatement or overstatement.

Write about the process of writing a short story—the original impression, inspiration, and thought, the talking to the mirror or typewriter to push you along, and so forth.

Live what you write about (but in writing). That is, become the person you write about or re-create; this, as better to understand her/him as a character or a subject.

Write a new proverb (one that is suggested by an old one) and accompany it with an explanation of its origin and meaning.

For various basic techniques of creative writing, study and imitate one or more of the following: Byron, Cervantes, Chekhov, Crane, De Crevecoeur, Jonathan Edwards, T.S. Eliot, Solomon Goldman, Hardy, Hawthorne, Poe, Shakespeare, John Smith the pilgrim captain, Solzhenitsyn, Tolstoy, Twain, Welty, Whitman.

CRITICAL WRITING

What Critical Writing Is

Generally, critical writing sets out to evaluate or to analyze a work of art. This analysis may be attempted in any number of ways, but for our purposes here we will divide critical writing into its two basic types—the theoretical and the practical. The theoretical concerns itself with general notions about the value of art as a whole (see Aristotle's *Poetics*, to cite one classic example), while the practical evaluates particular works, writers, styles, and so forth, in terms of whatever esthetic theory the critic may hold. Critical writing has encompassed nearly every literary form imaginable, from Plato's dialogues, through Horace's verse, to Keats' letters, Arnold's essays, and, more recently still, the applied psychological techniques of a critic like I.A. Richards. Our century has also seen other nonliterary disciplines brought to bear upon literary criticism—the Marxist dialectic, for example, or Freudian analysis. Some contemporary critics— Edmund Wilson was one—have combined various critical approaches (for example, biographical, textual, impressionistic) to illuminate a work and bring it home to the reader.

How to Write Criticism

It will be evident from the above that critical writing is another mode difficult to get a firm grasp on. Probably the beginning critic should settle for a simple analysis of the content and form of a story, novel or poem and an evaluation of how the form and content work, or fail to work, together to achieve the desired effect. He or she would do well to stick closely to the work at hand and to document rigorously from that text any criticisms made. This disciplined approach should eventually make for concrete, vigorously thought-out, and fully felt critical writing and be valuable for other types of writing as well. It might also be wise to let the specific critical approach—or combination of approaches—be dictated as definitively as possible by the work itself. For an obviously autobiographical novel, James Joyce's *A Portrait of the Artist as a Young Man*, a biographical tack might be of some value. A historical epic such as Sigrid Undset's *Kristin Lavransdatter* would clearly call, however, for a different approach.

Locating Subjects for Critical Writing

The topics in this section were listed primarily with literary criticism in mind. However, many of them may be applied to criticism in other disciplines—music, painting, film, architecture, photography, almost anything. The themes here generally lend themselves to practical criticism, rather than the theoretical. This is the type of criticism most students would be called upon to write and also the type they would most likely come upon in newspapers and magazines. Some of the questions in the chapter on cause and effect (see especially pages 43 through 45) might lend themselves to critical writing of a more theoretical variety.

We have seen many times over how thoroughly the kinds of writing outlined in this book are related. This is especially true of critical writing. Even research-and-report writing—which some people treat nowadays like a stuffy old uncle dottering out behind the stacks—assumes an important place here. A survey of almost any library's collection of critical works will reveal that some of the most exacting and often vitally written criticism has been scholarly. Process, classification/division, exposition, argumentation, definition, creative writing—any one of these is of rudimentary value in writing criticism. In fact, this seems an appropriate place to end this book. A working familiarity with the kinds of writing dealt with before will cement a reliable foundation on which to write critically. Not, one would hope, to mock and tear, but to carry forward for us all the wonder and love of language.

Common Themes in Literature for Critical Analysis

adventure

adversity

aging and the aged

alcoholism

alienation

ambiguity/ambivalence

ambition

animals

appearance vs. reality

aristocracy

art and artists

beauty

beliefs and customs

betrayal

Biblical types

birth, fertility, and rebirth

boredom and malaise

bribery

bureaucracy

capital punishment

change and progress

chaos

charity

childlikeness, childishness, and immaturity

children

choice and decision

Christ, Christ complex, Christianity, and martyr complex

civilization

clergy

code-living

common destiny

communication (or lack of it)

community (or lack of it)

complacency

comprehensiveness and infinity

confession

conflict

conscience

conservatism

consolation

convention

conversion

counterparts and counterpoints

country vs. city

courage and cowardice

cruelty and violence

curse

dance

danger

death

deduction

defeat and failure

demons and devils

dependence

depression, despair, discontent, and disillusionment

destruction and destructiveness

determinism, chance, fortune, fate, and indifferent universe

devotion

discovery, including self-discovery

divorce

domination, enslavement, and suppression

dope and dope addiction

double-character, analogue, and reflection of self in others

dreaming, dreams, imaginings, and fancies

duty

emotional disturbance

envy

epiphany

escape

evil eye

exile

expediency

exploitation

faith and loss of faith

falsity, pretense, and artificiality

fame

family, fatherhood, and motherhood

fanaticism

farming

Faust(ianism)

fear and terror

folly

free will and will power

freedom

Freudianism

frugality

fulfillment

gambling

games, contests, sports, competition, and trickery

God and Creation

God and Humanity

Godliness

good and evil, goodness, sin, and virtue

greed

grief and remorse

grotesquerie

guilt

happiness

heaven, including paradise on earth

hell
helplessness
heroes, heroines, and leaders
holiday
home
hospitality and offense to community
human and animal
humanity and human understanding
hunting
hypnotism
hypocrisy and duplicity
ideality, perfection, and exemplariness
identity
illusion and innocence
imprisonment
independence
initiation, experience, manhood, and womanhood
instinct vs. reason and heart vs. reason
jealousy
journey, travel, excursion, and voyage, including
    psychological journey
killing and murder
law
learning, schooling, and knowledge
leave-taking
life, *joie de vivre*, and life spirit
loneliness and aloneness
love and affection
loyalty
luck machine vs. humanity
marriage
master/servant and employer/employee
materialism
memory
metaphysical experience
militarism and military life
mind and matter
miracle
mischief
mob psychology
moral code
music and song
the mysterious stranger
mystery
natural force and natural disaster
nature and humanity
obsession, monomania, compulsion, and habit
optimism
pacifism
parent and child relationship; adult and child relationship
past-present-future

patriotism
persistence and perseverance
politics
poverty
prejudice
pride
primitivism
profession
promise
prophecy
prostitution
race and racial attitudes
reality and realness
reincarnation and immortality
religion
repentance
rescue
resistance, rebellion, and revolution
respectability
responsibility
return
revenge and retribution
ritual
rivalry
sacrifice
sadism/masochism
sanity, insanity, and senility
scapegoat and victim
seafaring
search
secrecy and secret world
sexuality and sexual conquest
sickness and the invalid
social status
societal or cultural differences
societal pressures
sophistication
soul and soul mates
spiritual crisis
stoicism
suicide
supernatural, magic, fairies, and ghosts
survival
suspicion
theft and ransom
time and circumstances, timelessness, eternity,
    time and space
tolerance
tradition and insularity
unity and human solidarity
universality and microcosm

value/value system

war

the wasted life, the empty life

wealth and the wealthy

womanhood, feminism, and the rights of women

youth

AUTHOR

David Powell received his BA, MA, and PhD degrees respectively from San Francisco State University, New Mexico Highlands University, and Southern Illinois University. He began teaching in 1959 and since 1970 has been teaching at Western New Mexico University, where he serves as Chair of the Department of Language and Literature. He has been a reviewer, writer, translator, or editor of numerous scholarly publications.

M. D. La Mar
712 El Camino Corvo
Prescott, AZ 86301